MW01492625

2093 Philadelphia Pike #8185

Claymont, DE 19703

ISBN: 9781795769723

This is a work of creative nonfiction. All events are portrayed to the best of Danielle Dempsey's memory. No one's memory is perfect, so in cases where the author has forgotten specific details such as colors, the author has inserted fiction to make up for these gaps. Some events have been compressed into one for the sake of short story telling. The conversations in the book are not meant to be taken as word-for-word transcripts. However, in all cases, the dialogue is accurate in its essence of emotion and how it was received by Danielle in her recollections. Some names and environmental details have been changed to protect individual's privacy.

To my mother, who taught me what it means to be resilient.

To my father, who instilled in me the work ethic that allowed me to finish writing this book, despite stopping many times.

To my brothers, I love you and I am proud of you.

To my husband, who after each accidental spill of some wild childhood story, you only loved me more. You are my safehouse.

To you, the reader, as much as misery loves company, so does healing love camaraderie. Hello, friend.

BEHIND THE WHITE PICKET FENCE

A collection of memories.

NOTE FROM THE AUTHOR:

Some names have been changed to protect individual's privacy. My story is my own and I am committed to telling the truth to the best of my ability. Including things that embarrass myself- because frankly sometimes that's what happens.

I wish not to hurt anyone, but in the words of Anne Lamott, "If people wanted you to write warmly about them, they should have behaved better".

So, to those who are mentioned in this book: I hope you like your fictional name.

Table of Contents

No, Don't Do That!

(13 years old)

A boisterous thud comes from the coffee table and I wander towards it to investigate. Luke's yell followed by Joe's laugh greet me upon arrival. On the floor, my brothers are engaged in an all-out brawl. The rowdy display forces my eyebrows inward, my eyes dancing over the scene. I don't think I've ever seen my brothers wrestle before.

Luke is struggling to break free from Joe's hold which has him pinned roughly to the ground. The fight is far from fair, considering Joe is twice the size of Luke. Still, Luke thrashes desperately in search of the upper hand. Both breathe heavy with intermittent laughs breaking the tension.

I stand there, following their movements. Boys wrestle, it's a totally normal thing to do. Yet, the longer I watch, the tighter my chest becomes. Like a boa constrictor closing in for the kill, the pressure becomes unignorable. My breathing quickens, and I fight to keep it steady.

Not again.

They're grabbing at each other by whatever means necessary to win. Joe's on top. Luke's on top. It's innocent, I tell myself. They're having fun. This is what brothers do.

But the yell is climbing up my throat. Its nails jabbing into my esophagus forcing its way to my lips. The panic is setting in. The fear is washing over me.

"Stop! Stop! That's inappropriate! You shouldn't touch each other like that."

My brothers look up at me with surprise, embarrassment reddening their faces as they separate. Shame forces my eyes to the ground. I have perverted their fun.

Behind me my mother's footsteps hurry into the room, "What is going on in here?"

"They were being inappropriate!" My words are rushed, my voice unsure.

"No, they were just wrestling. That perfectly normal, Danielle. Leave them alone."

My mother returns to the room from which she came, her heavy sigh trailing behind her. When I hear her plop back into her office chair, I slowly walk over to the couch without looking up.

Joe and Luke continue playing, but they don't wrestle anymore. I don't dare to see what game they play now, as my cheeks are still hot, and my heart rate has only slightly slowed. I know my words are still echoing in their ears. They're still echoing in mine.

I pull my knees to my chest and squeeze my eyes shut. Frustration furrows my brows as I crush myself into the smallest shape I can muster and search for responses to my ever-present question.

What is wrong with me?

The answers I'm looking for swim away as soon as I reach out to grab them. I let them escape and sit unmoving, afraid of what the fleetingness of my memory is hiding from me.

My mother enters the room again and glances at my tightly compacted figure. She walks past with a simple command. "Meet me in your room."

Peeling my skin from the leather, I slink off the couch and follow her. In my room, she sits tall on my bed and pats the space next to her. I follow her silent instruction, crossing my legs beneath me.

"Are you sure nothing ever happened at Grandma and Grandpa's?"

"No!"

I thrust the word at her, but it falls out jumbled and frantic. She's asked me this question before, anytime I lose control. Anytime the outbursts and meltdowns are too strong to suppress.

My mouth twists in disgust at the idea that something bad happened to me. But the swimming answers shimmer at me beneath the murky lake of my memory and I pause.

"Not that I can remember."

Guilt surrounds my answer. I can't find the cause of my hurt, so it sounds like the truth, but it feels like a lie. There's something there. Something I should be able to remember, but I just can't reach.

I look up and she searches my eyes. I don't know what she is looking for, but the worry on her face makes me search again. And again. And again.

Locked in the Bathroom

(4 Years Old)

My mother, grandmother and I sit in a Red Robin red leather booth. When I was told we'd be eating here I practically jumped out of my seat with joy. But the longer we sit, the less thrilled I become. My appetite abandons me so I just stare at my food, watching it get cold.

"Come on Beth, let us take her to Sedona. She wants to go!" my grandmother's eyes are intense. Unapologetically, she inflicts wounds with guilt wrenching words until my mother is squirming in her seat.

The idea of going on a vacation alone with her and my grandfather puts knots in my stomach that threaten to make me vomit. But the look in her eyes beg me to comply. She's a very petite woman whose skin has grown frail with age. I think of all the pills she swallows just to buy another day. Her eyes are dark with sadness and a vacancy I don't think anyone has ever been able to fill. "I love you so much, doodlebug." Her words echo in my ears.

My mother bites her lip and looks down at me.

She's debating whether to stand her ground or give up. I've seen this look before. I stare back at her with blank eyes, while my stomach and heart compete. One doing flips while the other palpitates.

"Do you want to go, Danielle?"

My mother's question carries a sort of pleading. I feel her willing me to say no, but I can't speak. Safety sits sweetly beside my mother, whispering my name. But Obligation and Empathy each grab an arm and yank me towards my grandmother. Torn between them, my voice has run and hid.

"Of course, she does." My grandmother quickly answers, certain she will get her way.

They both turn their attention to me. Their gazes hold me firm in my seat, the red leather slowly devouring me. The tension is closing in, cutting off my air and shrinking me three sizes smaller. I try to break their eye contact, but they hold firm. This won't end until I give them an answer. But which answer I give will determine how long this continues. I need this friction to end, and I know who will cave more easily. I know how to make it stop.

A whisper escapes my lips, "Mom, Grandma really

wants me to go."

And with that, it's decided. My grandmother's smug smile makes me visibly cringe and I put a cold fry in my mouth to prevent further discussion.

. . .

During the drive to Sedona, my grandmother points out the red rock all around. "Isn't it beautiful?"

I nod to appease her, but truthfully, the city gives off a sort of eeriness that I can't shake. Or maybe just being alone with my grandparents gives me the creeps. I don't know if I can tell the difference anymore.

The roads turn to gravel as we drive into a trailer park. We pull into our lot and the crushing sound of gravel hushes as the truck is parked where it will stay for the next week. The sudden sound of silence booms reminding me of one thing. I am miles from the safety of my mother. I am alone.

My grandmother twists words and bends wills, but she never hurts me and often she buys me gifts. So, she doesn't seem so awful. But every muscle in my body tenses when my grandfather is around. His smile is wicked and sinister. His hands always beckoning, always motioning for me to sit on his lap and give him a kiss.

While conniving, my grandmother's side is the safest place on this trip. So, I take up residence there. Time to make lunch? I'll get the plates. Grandma needs to change? I'll pick out the shirt. I attach myself to her, my closeness second only to her shadow. When we walk, I slink past my grandfather careful to avoid his touch and his stare.

My plan seems foolproof and I stand up tall, proud of my cleverness. That is until my grandmother kneels to meet my height.

"Grandma is going to go take the dogs for a walk. Stay here, okay?"

"I can help!"

"No, stay here with your grandpa." I look over to where he sits on the pull-out bed. Smile creepily growing.

"Please let me come with you" I beg.

"I'll just be a minute."

"Let her go. Come over here." My grandfather's booming voice freezes my body motionless.

He's a large man. Loud and commanding, his presence is rarely ignored by family and strangers alike. No one questions a man with a smug smile and sure-fire confidence. His word is law and with that my grandmother slips out of the camper door. My eyes account each step that carriers her further and further away until she's out of yelling range.

"Shut that door. Leave your grandmother alone and come over here." The monster behind me instructs. His tone is strong, but sweet enough to cover the threatening behind it.

Fear washes over me, but I don't move. My eyes stay fixated on my grandmother as I watch her walk out of sight. My heart reaches out to her, longing for her safety to return.

This is all my fault. I tired her out. My clinginess has suffocated her, and now she needs a break. Singlehandedly, I have trapped myself with the monster of a man she married.

Slowly, reluctantly, I shut the door. The bed behind me squeaks, sending shivers racing down my spine and I whip around to look at him. Pulling one leg onto the bed, he catches my gaze and motions me over. His eyes are fierce and expecting.

Thoughts fly through my head at lightning speed. I look left then right. Searching for an escape, the ajar bathroom door catches my attention. I race inside, locking the door behind me. He curses and thuds over to where I hide.

"Danielle, open this door right now."

My breaths are short and quick. Tears begin to pool, and I shake my head. He can't see my response, but the words won't come.

His fist connects with the door again, shaking the tiny bathroom and I jump. Tiptoeing towards the door to check the lock, I stop and stare at myself in the mirror. I demand courage to show on my face, but the only thing I see is the crippling fear I feel inside.

"I want to make sure you're okay, let me in." His words are sugary and pleasant this time.

"I'm going to the bathroom! You can't come in here!"

He grumbles, and his footsteps make their way back to the bed. Filled with brief relief, my legs give, and I slump to the ground. The toilet offers a less than comfortable headrest, but it is favorable to the alternative. Holding my knees to my chest, I look down at my feet. I'm stuck.

I turn my focus to the door's lock and pray it

doesn't magically come undone and let the monster in. "Please hurry, please hurry" I try to send a mental SOS to my grandmother. The minutes passing feel like hours.

"Are you sure you're okay in there?" My grandfather calls again. Frustration coating his voice.

"I'm going poop!" I try to keep my voice steady. I need to buy more time and I'm afraid if he senses my fear, he will bust down the door.

Finally, I hear the camper door open and my grandmother announces her return. I release the breath I hadn't realized I'd been holding and push myself to my feet. Turning on the faucet, I wash my hands to carry out my lie. When I emerge from the bathroom my grandfather shoots daggers of discipline and anger at me. I flinch as though they pierce through my skin.

My grandmother, unaffected by the tension, asks what we should have for dinner. And all is normal again.

. . .

After the longest week of my life, I'm dropped off at home to my mother's open arms, hugs and kisses. I am grateful to be home, but my soul tingles with numbness. My mother's embrace feels nothing more than an empty touch. I stay stiff, gripping onto the stuffed animal my grandparents bought for me. Another present to keep me happy, to keep me coming back.

"Did you have fun?"

"Sure. It made Grandma really happy"

I don't look at her when I answer. Instead, I place the stuffed animal on my bed, making silent promises to myself. Never again will I be alone with them. Never again will I let the guilt of being a good granddaughter force me so far from safety. Never again.

"Are you okay?" my mother asks, the same fear in her eyes that was in me during my bathroom quarantine.

"Yeah."

The word falls flat. I search for more emotion to show, but I have none left. So, instead I sit on my bed, a terrified empty shell of a girl, and just stare at the wall.

Kick Him While He's Down

(6 Years Old)

My brothers and I wait in the living room, while our grandmother finishes getting ready. We're supposed to be going out to eat.

Joe and I are bickering as usual. No longer the baby in the family he seems to have a lot of attitude lately. Being the oldest, I'm supposed to rise above it. But I don't always. My anger boils and we yell at each other relentlessly. In frustration, I huff, cross my arms and throw myself onto the couch. It's then that my grandmother walks into the living room, makeup fresh and ready to go.

"Finally!" I head towards the door and Joe kicks me as I walk by. "Ow!"

When I turn to him, he wears a smug grin. Behind me, my grandfather's face glows a deep red, irritation radiating. Unaware of his reaction, we continue bickering while walking down the steps of the trailer. Just as I am about to spat another insult, my grandfather's foot connects squarely with Joe's back.

"Treat others how you want to be treated!" he bellows

Joe tumbles down the trailer steps hitting the sizzling Arizona concrete with a solid thud.

"Harold!" my grandmother scolds but doesn't move or saying anything else.

When the color returns to my cheeks, I slowly walk over to where Joe is still lying on the ground. His eyes grab onto mine, shock and fear registering on his face. I pull him up and brush the dirt from his clothes. He doesn't seem to have any visible injuries, but the most painful trauma is rarely seen on the outside. My grandfather grunts and continues walking towards the truck, unbothered by the altercation. Joe and I stand together now as wide-eyed, unmoving lawn ornaments, staring at our grandfather.

"Come on! Get in the truck!" His words crackle in the air, giving life to our bones once again. Silently, we crawl into the cab of the truck as my grandfather slams every door he touches.

. . .

When our visit is over, we rigidly rest on the couch, awaiting our mother's return. Only the floor boards speak, single high pitch creaks with every heavy step that takes my grandfather over to the recliner across from me. Is my grandfather allowed to kick us? Can he do that?

My mother arrives and we're about to leave when I begin to open my mouth. But as soon as the smallest sound leaves my lips, I am stopped by my grandfather's glare. His taut lips and squinted eyes challenge me. The intensity and assurance of retaliation reaches out, grabbing my lips and closing them shut.

My eyes dart from my mother's expectant look to my grandfather's warning scowl and I shake my head dismissively. Turning away, I know I have failed Joe. The most important responsibility of an older sister out of my grasp. My grandfather is a monster I can't conquer. We all wish to be heroes, but in this moment, I am nothing but a silent bystander, a fear muzzled mutt.

Joe and I look at each other, knowingly. I have failed him, and our grandfather has failed us both.

In the Oven

(8 Years Old)

"Danielle, talk to me." My mother's voice is thick with hurt.

"I don't have anything to say." My gaze is fixated on the bathroom mirror, my head held high with indignation as the wall inside my heart grows taller. Her pleas run into it and fall onto the ground of our broken relationship.

The silence lingers while she watches me finish brushing my hair. When I turn to push past her, she blocks the door with her body. "Danielle. You *have* to talk to me. I'm your mother."

"I don't *have* to talk to anyone. My words are my own. It is my decision when I will use them." I stand up straighter, furious and defiant. "You might be able to stop me from seeing grandma, but you can't force me to speak."

I think back to the nights when my grandmother would call, the pink cellphone she gave me quietly buzzing underneath my pillow where I kept it hidden.

"Don't worry Doodlebug, if you hear your mom coming just hang up and pretend to sleep." She would whisper.

"I'm really not supposed to be on the phone grandma. Not this late at night. Mom will get mad."

"Don't worry about her. She's just mad at me, not you. She isn't being fair."

With every secret conversation my disdain for my mother grew. In the fight for my heart, my grandmother had won.

I cross my arms, my blue eyes blazing with outrage. For a moment we just stand there, staring. A silent mental chess game taking place. Until finally, my mother's head slumps and she lets me walk past.

It's been almost a month since I last saw my grandmother. The anger has made camp in my soul. Even the cool autumn breeze doesn't dim the fire as I walk outside to escape my mother's watch.

The whole neighborhood has started a football game in the middle of the street. They all laugh at their failed attempts and skinned knees. Taking turns hiking the ball, they run several fake plays. The obvious fun has my attention and I'm about to join in when a familiar voice calls my name.

I look over to the front porch of our house. When I see him, my father turns and walks back inside - his cue for me to follow.

As I walk through the yard, the grass crunches beneath my feet. Each step so heavy it sends a vibration through my body. I raise my walls a little bit higher, in anticipation of the lecture I am about to receive.

When I reach the living room, my mother is sitting in the black massage chair on the far right. My father is perched on the dull pink sectional opposite of her. We had used those pink cushions to build many forts, but his facial expression is far from one of fort-making playfulness. Sitting in front of the TV, in the middle of the room, was one of the yellow wood chairs from our kitchen table. The perfect set up for an interrogation.

"Sit down, Danielle." My mother requests. Her voice is cool and collected, but her eyes are red.

I plop into the chair with enough attitude to fill two teenagers, more attitude than my eight-year-old body should be able to handle.

"Obviously, this isn't working. So, we are going to tell you what is going on." My mother continues.

I look from her to my father. Confusion written on my face, anticipation keeping me silent.

"Your grandparents' aren't good people, that's why we aren't seeing them anymore. They are mean and manipulative. They're dangerous."

"What are you talking about?" I rush to my grandmother's defense whom I'd been conditioned to view as the victim.

"They're crazy, Danielle. I used to have to vacuum every day and if the lines weren't perfectly straight, I would be beaten."

"You're pretty strict about how we clean things too, mom" I counter.

She sighs, "Let's put it this way. Instead of time out, when I would get in trouble, they would take all the shelves out of the oven, force me to get in, shut the door and threaten to turn it on!" Her voice is louder now, shaking.

Shock pushes my mouth open. Tears are pricking my eyes; my throat is swelling with every word.

"No. You're wrong."

My mother's seriousness intensifies, "I am telling

you the truth. They *will* hurt you. I am just trying to protect you!"

I shake my head aggressively in denial. All the while, my father sits silently on his side of the room, watching my mother's eyes fill with tears and then looking at mine.

"Is it true?" I ask him. Hoping he will contradict her and say she's making it out worse than it really is, 'Dramatic as usual'.

"Your mother wants to protect you. She grew up with them and she's realizing more and more. They could do the same things to you." His face is somber.

I look at the ground. My mind is bouncing. Grappling with my memories, I try to rectify the many versions of my grandmother that exist in my mind. After a moment, I look back at my mother who is crying, and the walls begin to crumble. I've been shutting out the wrong woman.

"You guys think I'm strict on how I make you clean the house. But I am nowhere near as strict or horrible as my parents were to me. My parents threw dishes and broke things-" her voice faulters.

Now I'm crying. I want to hug my mother, but I

can't move. My chest is tight, and my throat has closed in on itself. A soft, barely audible "okay" is the only thing I can push out.

"Are you okay?" my mother asks through her sadness.

I nod and stop the tears from falling. "Can I go play now?"

My mother's eyes widen with confusion. She looks at my father who studies me for a minute before saying, "Sure".

With disappointment and grief firmly squatting on my shoulders, I use both my hands to push myself forward and off of the wooden chair. My legs wobble when I try to stand, but I head towards the door anyway. I make it into the kitchen before I hear my mother begin to weep. The sound stops me for a moment, but pride propels me forward.

As if the world has turned to slow motion, all noises muffle. The vibration of my every step resonates within my bones. I feel only the pressure of the ground move from the heel of my foot to the ball, as I reach the front door. My surroundings blurred; my world spinning; I don't pause for even a second. Through the front yard and into the street, I look around.

The impromptu football game is still going and has been undisturbed by my revelation. I watch as Claire falls while trying to catch the ball. They all rush to her, but I stay where I am. My feet glued to the asphalt, I don't hear my name called.

"Danielle!" the neighbor girl yells again. "Are you okay?"

Everyone is looking at me now. I'm immobile, staring at them for just a moment before catching sight of my brothers in my peripheral. I smile wide. My brothers have no idea the things my grandparents are capable of and I'll be damned if they learn. I wipe my face from any evidence of tears and push all other thoughts out of my mind.

"Yeah, I'm great! Mom and Dad just had a question. Can I join you guys?"

Running Away

(9 Years Old)

My head turns quickly in both directions. I scan the aisle up and down. My mother is gone. I start heading towards the end of the aisle and look to the right and then the left. No luck. I walk over to the milk and strike out again. I pick up a little speed as I head to the produce. Not there either. No one offers to try to help me find my mother, but I attract a lot of stares. "Maybe she's looking for me and we're going in circles" I think to myself as I double back to where I started.

With slow, deliberate steps I make my way to where my search began, taking in my surroundings in case I find her on my way back. I walk past several other customers who look my way.

There's a woman with a small child, he's begging to put Oreos in the shopping cart. The woman is rubbing her head and I can almost hear her sigh from across the aisle. There are three teenagers giggling at each other, as they reach for different flavored Peace Teas. A middle-aged man places a bag of lettuce in his cart, probably grabbing groceries for his wife on his way home from work.

The seconds have grown into minutes and I still haven't found my mother. I can hear my heartbeat in my ears as I soothe myself by repeating that all these people are safe. I am safe. They're just getting groceries. They're just living their lives, no need to fear. I repeat this to myself as I focus on taking even breaths. The time apart from my mother grows greater. I spot another shopper walking towards me. This man is older, around the age of my grandfather. I tilt my chin up slightly to look at his face. The wrinkles on his face cascade over his protruding check bones. I see him staring at me as we walk toward each other and begin to try and memorize his description, you know, in case he tries to kidnap me, and I have to file a police report.

It's okay, I'm safe, I tell myself. Another few steps closer. It's okay, I'm safe. Three more steps. It's okay, I'm safe.

I try to force myself to keep walking, but everything in me screams to run. I repeat to myself that I'm safe like my mother taught me. Keep calm, don't overreact. My internal battle rages on and he continues to look at me. He's probably just wondering why I'm alone. I try and reason the fear away. Or is he staring at me as his next victim? Evil can hide in the most unlikely places. I feel something inside yanking me another direction. He raises an eyebrow at me and my breath catches.

A chord of fear in my soul is struck so strong it resonates throughout my body. Its force propels my legs to run without my permission. I race past him and zig zag through the aisles. I don't dare look back, if the man has followed me the sight of him would quickly render me still. I run until I almost slam straight into my mother.

"What are you doing?" she asks.

"I lost you." I say in a quiet voice

Safe by my mother's side, I look around for the evil old man. He's nowhere to be found and the fear subsides. But disappointment rushes to take its place. When will I stop running? When will I stop being afraid? I overreacted. Again. That fact alone is enough to fill me with shame as I stay quiet on the car ride home.

Pen Pal

(11 years old)

"Now, when you write a letter, you want to address all their questions first, and then ask your own." My mother instructs.

My leg bounces underneath my sleek, white desk, anxious to begin. I'm responding to a letter my father's mother wrote me. I just recently learned of this hidden grandmother and I am giddy at the thought of a replacement for my mother's parents whom I haven't seen in over two years. I picture her in a small apartment in California where she lives. I imagine that she has short, curly white hair like the grandmas on TV and a sweet smile. Perhaps she is the kind of grandma who always pinches your cheeks or the kind that always has freshly baked cookies.

My mother grabs an envelope and points to the upper left corner. "This is where you will put our address. I'll give it to you later." Her finger moves to the center of the envelope, "This is where your grandma's address will go".

"Okay I've got it, I've got it." I push her aside and

get busy writing. I fill the page with questions about where she lives and what she does for fun. I get pretty good at it and before I know it, I'm writing her a few times a month.

. . .

Today, when I get home from school, another letter is waiting on the counter for me. My heart swells, happy to have someone to fill the void that had been glaring at me. Every time a friends' grandparents picked them up from school early or came to their birthday parties, I was reminded of the hand my family had been dealt. Us, me, alone against the world. But not anymore. Now, we had Grandma LeAnne.

I pick up the letter and turn it over in my hands. I try to soak up every ounce of it, solidifying the connection we had been building. My fingertip reaches underneath the white flap and I'm about to rip it open like every time before, when something catches my eye.

In large red letters, I see "Federal State Prison" inked over the flag stamp in the top right corner. My eyebrows furrow. I squint my eyes to make sure I'm reading it correctly. I re-read it again. "Federal State Prison". I stare at the envelope intently and search my memory. Like an unbearably slow elevator, my heart sinks to my stomach. The horrifying details of my mother's parents and the strike against seeing them comes rushing back. Dread pats me on the back and I fear another conversation looming in the distance.

Cautiously, with one foot in front of the other, I walk to my room. The bed makes a "poof" sound as I jump onto it, my eyes never leaving the upper right corner of the envelope. My body sinks deeper into the mattress and my mind deeper in thought.

We've been getting along so well. Do I just pretend I don't see it? Maybe if I just keep writing her, it won't matter. But what if my parents change their mind? Has this stamp always been here? How have I not seen it before?

I need answers. I get up from my bed and walk across the hall to the home office where my mother is organizing.

"Why does Grandma's letter say, 'Federal State Prison' on it?"

The words are out of my mouth before she realizes I'm there. Her hand stops in the middle of tossing a paper onto the floor. Her eyes widen, reflecting back my concern. Stray pieces of hair fall out of her ponytail as she weighs my question and no doubt her answer.

"You're going to need to ask your father that when he gets home."

The dismissal shocks me. I wait for her to say more, but she doesn't. She simply resumes throwing pieces of trash onto the floor.

When I return to my room, I don't open the letter. Instead, I set it on my desk. It appears even more daunting now that it perches alone on the stark white material. The envelope taunts me, and my eyes stay locked on it like a missile with a target.

I don't know how long I sit, just staring at the letter, before I finally hear my father's footsteps enter the house. I wait a moment and listen for where they carry him. I pray he comes straight to my room, but he doesn't. Afraid my mother might have forgotten to ask him, I rush to receive my answers. When I find him, he's standing with my mother in the kitchen. They both look at me, jolted and unsure. My eagerness fades and I take a step back and wait for them to say something. The silence stretches for miles.

"Well?" I ask.

My father straightens, "We're going to have a

family meeting. Go back to your room. I will come and get you when it's time."

. . .

We're all sitting at the long wooden table in the dining room. The benches that replace typical dining chairs feel more uncomfortable than usual. My parents don't sit, instead they stand at the head of the table. My brothers look from me to my father. I look from my father to them.

"Alright. It's about time you guys know this. Danielle got a letter from my mom and it has a Federal Prison stamp on it. The stamp is on there because that is where she lives."

I could've guessed that, but my heart sinks at the confirmation anyway. My brothers scrunch their noses and look at each other. Joe is eight and Luke is six. They haven't been writing to her, only me. This is an unprompted family meeting in their minds.

"Why is she in there?" I ask quietly. My voice as unsteady as my heart rate.

He sighs, looks down and clasps his hands together. "Your grandmother, my mom, is in prison because she was accused of murdering my father."

"What?" The word is carried on the breath that escapes me as if being punched in the gut.

He continues, "When I was young, just a little older than you Danielle, my dad was murdered. A friend of the family came into our home and stabbed him 37 times."

"But she wasn't the one who killed him?" I ask looking for her redemption.

"They believe my mom had a relationship with him and convinced him to murder my father." He pauses, "So, she's in prison for planning it."

I sit in silence. It seems too theatrical to be real. How can this be? The woman I'd been corresponding with seemed so normal, so loving. How could she have done something so horrific? How can so much darkness be in the world? How can so much of it be in my own family?

"Do you think she did it?" I can't stop myself. I need more answers.

"Alright, that's enough." My mother tries to step in, glancing at my father whose face looks grimmer by the second. But my father sees the search in my eyes.

"I don't know."

An emptiness overcomes me and I'm out of

questions. I look at both of my parents. Two loving, caring people, both born and raised out of such evil. I don't get it.

My brothers and I are asked if we have any questions. When we all shake our heads, we're dismissed.

I clench and unclench my jaw while walking back to my room. I pull out a piece of paper and write back to my grandmother. I follow my mom's instructions and respond to all her questions first. When it is my turn to ask questions, I only have one.

"Today I saw the stamp on your letter that says Federal Prison. Dad had to explain to us why it's there. Did you do it?" My hand stops writing. I don't know if I should ask, but I can't make myself take it back. So, I continue, *"Even if you did, I forgive you. I love you grandma."*

Perhaps it's easy to forgive her because I didn't know my grandfather. Maybe, I am just so desperate for a normal family I'm willing to look the other way. Or maybe, it's just denial. Either way, I wait a month for a response, but one doesn't come. Another month passes then another and another.

Not Good Enough

(12 Years Old)

My mirror is extremely dusty. I cock my head slightly to the right to get a better look. How does it get so dirty? I focus on a few water spots, considering where they came from. Then my mind shifts from the dirtiness of the mirror to my body. I've stripped down to just my bra and underwear. It's as far as I can go. I reach to unbuckle my bra. What do I look like? But my hand faulters before it reaches the clasp. I'm afraid of what I will see.

I turn from side to side, examining my shape and thinness. I'm petite. Everyone says so. They mention constantly how lucky I am. But my eyes don't light up with joy at the skinny girl in front of me. Instead, in the back of my mind the words echo, "Not good enough." My mind travels back to last Sunday at church.

Mia runs up to me on stage. We're practicing worship before service starts. "Hey Danielle, I just heard something you're not going to believe!" I stare cautiously at the girl who I know isn't any friend of mine. What could she possibly have to tell me?

"I just overheard Grayson's parents talking about you." My heart skips a beat at the mention of his name. "They said they can't believe he would like someone like you. They said Grayson is way too good for you."

My heart sinks, "You're lying."

"No, I'm not! I'm not that mean!"

I look over to where Grayson's mom and dad are talking to each other. I see them glance in my direction and my eyes drop to the floor.

It was only a few days later when Grayson texted me and said he couldn't talk to me anymore. Thrown out like garbage is what lead to this staring contest with myself.

Now, standing squarely in the mirror, my eyes start at my feet and travel up until I am looking myself in the eyes. I scan my face for some sort of sign. No one could seem to tell me why Grayson's parents didn't like me, and I couldn't remember anything I'd done. I take a step closer to the mirror and look harder for where my worthiness lacks but come up empty. Again. I ball my hands into fists and look away. I can't stand to see myself for a second longer.

Glancing at the clock, I notice time has passed

much quicker than I thought, and the school bus will be here any minute. I rush to get dressed, brush my hair and throw on a pair of shoes. In a hurry, I skip breakfast on the way out like I've done several times before. But today when we're dismissed for lunch, I don't eat then either. And when I get home and my mother says dinner is ready, I lie and say I had a big lunch.

"I'm not hungry, can I go to my room? I have a lot of homework."

My mother raises an eyebrow at me but agrees. I hurry to my room and shut the door. I am as shocked as her that I don't eat dinner, but my appetite has forsaken me and I'm not in the mood for food.

The next morning, I wake up disheartened. I put on my brown, wired frame glasses and walk over to the full-length mirror in the corner of my room. I stare and wonder once again. Am I not nice enough? Not funny enough? Not smart enough? My face looks grimmer than yesterday.

I put on my clothes and leave for school. Today, I skip lunch again, but I eat a little bit of dinner. Just a few bites before saying, "I ate another big lunch today, can I be dismissed?" My mother worryingly agrees, and I head to my room. I jump onto my bed and with my earbuds in,

I listen to sad music as loud as I can stand. I let my mind go blank as I stare at the ceiling and let the music take over.

It's Friday and my friends are starting to ask me questions. "Are you okay?" "Why aren't you talking to anyone?" "How come you aren't eating lunch?"

"I'm just tired." "I don't have anything to say." "I ate a big breakfast." I lie through every accusation that comes my way. I don't know what I'm feeling, all I know is I don't want to eat, talk or be around anyone. I just want to know what's wrong with me.

The weekend comes and goes. At church on Sunday, I notice Grayson's careful movements. How he quickly starts up a conversation with whoever is near-by when I pass him. I notice his parents coming in to pick him up and how his mother never smiles. I can feel her judgement and her disapproving face haunts my dreams. I feel worthless. A boy not liking me is one thing, but for his mom to think I'm not good enough, there must be a reason. Adults usually love me. Adults have good reasons for things.

Monday comes, and my friend Aurora and I are standing in line for lunch. "What are you going to have for lunch?" I ask, starting a conversation for the first time in a week.

"Probably pizza sticks, what about you?"

"I don't think I'll eat today." I tell her, my honesty surprising me. Until now, I had been quietly distracting others from my hunger strike. But something inside me shifts.

Suspicion narrows her eyes and she looks me over. "When's the last time you ate?"

I feel myself give in. Yes, it's terrible, but I want the attention. I want to know someone cares. I want someone to notice I'm starving myself. I want to feel loved, like I'm not some major waste of life just walking around in a daze.

"Probably Tuesday."

"Danielle! You need to eat! Why aren't you eating anything?!"

"I don't know"

It's a mostly honest answer. I didn't wake up and decide to stop eating, not really. I just kind of decided at each meal that I didn't want too.

"I don't need to eat, I've been doing fine. Besides I don't have any money for food. My mom thinks I'm supposed to be packing my lunch." I unzip my lunchbox to reveal its empty contents.

"Well you can have some of mine."

After going through the lunch-line, Aurora sits at our usual table with me and tells our friends I'm trying to skip lunch. Disbelieving scoffs, "you-should-know-betters" and various foods are shoved my direction.

"You're too beautiful to starve yourself." One of them informs me.

Their kind words and concern remind me I would hate to see any of them treat themselves the way I am treating myself. The haunting sadness doesn't disappear, but I eat. I look at my friends in front of me. They smile wide and laugh about trivial things. I must be doing something right to be surrounded by so much love. I feel a brief sense of okayness before a sinister voice hisses in the back of my mind.

"You'd deserve to eat, if you were good enough."

The food in my mouth becomes tasteless. I set what's in my hand down, and I don't eat the rest.

Isaac

(13 Years Old)

I'm alone sauntering through the school gates when I spot my best friend.

"Hey Addison!" She feigns a smile, but there's a storm behind her hazel eyes.

"What's wrong?"

"My brother started peeing blood the other day." I can see her mental expedition for an explanation, the emotional frustration seeping into her words.

"Um, I'm sure he'll be okay. It might just be a UTI, my mom gets them all the time. The doctors will give him some medicine and it'll be no big deal!" I effortlessly sprinkle my words with sugar to combat her sour.

It works, and her smile is sincerer this time. For the moment, her worries scurry away from the light. I loop my arm through hers and pull her close. We step in time towards class and distracting, carefully crafted stories begin to flow from my mouth.

A few weeks go by and Addison's absence becomes

increasingly apparent. Our classmates begin to notice and take to asking me questions. I give dismissive, undecisive answers to feign knowledge. But I have as many questions as they do, and more.

Addison doesn't find me when she returns to school. In fact, it's a few days before someone mentions seeing her and I realize she's been avoiding me.

"Hey! Addison!" I yell across the green, spotting her from several feet away. I run to catch up to her, "What's going on? Did I do something?"

She stares at the ground and soaks up my words. Then her eyes raise, looking into mine fiercely. "Isaac has cancer. It's some kind of cancer that only old men are supposed to get! It wasn't just a UTI."

Her words are sharp. I stumble backwards, wounded by her jab. We both stand there for a moment. Her eyes test me, and I am at a loss. I do the only thing I can think of and wrap my arms around her.

"I'm so sorry."

My grip tightens, and I try to squeeze some of the pain out. Desperately praying the pain leaves her and takes over me instead. It doesn't work. But what else can I do?

. . .

It's been several months, and Isaac is only getting weaker. We think, speak and pray positive, but the cloud looming over their home grows darker.

I champion my support for Addison as much as I can. I visit anytime her grandmother will let me through the door. Sometimes I bring my little brother Luke, who is Isaac's best friend. Other times my mother comes with me and talks with Addison's grandmother. But most of the time, it's just me. My coy attempt to ask where Addison's parents are gets shot down quickly and I see the twang of abandonment pile on top of her already overflowing hurt.

Today, Addison invites me in, and I notice the circles under her eyes. Her voice is a whisper of despair and she feels thinner when I hug her. Upon entering the living room, I notice Isaac isn't on the couch like he usually is. I'm surveying the scene when Addison's grandmother appears.

"Danielle, I'm glad you're here. Addison and I need to run to the store. Can you stay with Isaac?"

My mouth gapes, the entire English language abandoning me. I try my best to stuff down the fear and command my anxiety to hush.

"Um, sure. What do you guys need to get?"

I try to gauge how long I will have to be alone with him. There has never been a task asked of me that I was less prepared for than this.

"Just a few things, we won't be long". Walking across the living room she shows me into her bedroom where Isaac is laying, watching TV. "Isaac, Danielle is going to stay with you while Addison and I run to the store."

Isaac looks from his grandmother to me. I think I hear him say "okay", but I can't be sure. I notice how he doesn't even lift his head from the pillow. His skin clings to his bones, even more so than my last visit. His skin is three shades paler than mine. He'd look like a corpse already if it wasn't for his protruding belly, the only thing different between him and a science classroom skeleton.

I smile at him, "Hey bud, what have you been up too?"

"I'm just watching cartoons." He says looking back at the TV.

I realize how often he must get asked stupid, superficial questions like the one that just escaped my mouth.

"Cartoons? I love cartoons! Can I watch with you?" He smiles at me and I climb into the big bed next to him.

"Alright, we'll be back soon!" Addison's grandmother calls as she exits the bedroom.

The front door slams and I don't move an inch. Every muscle fiber in my body stays taut. I try to focus on the pictures on the screen, but my eyes glaze over. Several stretching minutes of ghost silence pass. Suddenly, Isaac speaks.

"Danielle, I'm scared. Can I hold your hand?"

I look at him and then back at the TV. This cartoon is far from scary, so I know he is talking about his circumstance.

My aching heart leaps into my throat and my eyes threatened to leak. "It's going to be okay" I say, reaching for his hand.

Except, I don't know that. I am lying for his sake. Or is it for mine? He smells of near death and his bones threaten to cut through his frail skin. His appearance is far from the playful young boy I knew a year ago. I'm afraid I'll break him. But looking back at me is a sweet young boy who is afraid of death.

This is the first time I've seen him afraid. He's been so positive, so strong. Either he's lost his confidence, or he has been putting on a show for his grandmother and sister. I relate to trying to keep your true feelings from those you love most, and my heart grows closer to his. Gingerly, I hold his hand, afraid it's going to crumble in my grasp. The tears in my eyes blur my vision but I blink them away.

"I like this cartoon a lot."

Isaac smiles and tells me he's already seen this episode. He begins to tell me the chain of events, but I can't focus on his words. My eyes are scanning his body and I look at the clock. Addison and her grandmother have been gone for twenty minutes. It dawns on me that if he needs any physical help, I won't be able to do it. This boy needs a full-time nurse at this point, and I am a 90 pound, 13-year-old girl.

Isaac stops talking and begins to make a long drawn out noise saturated with pain.

"I need to go to the bathroom."

"Uh, can you go by yourself?"

"No, I need help."

"Okay, um, I think your grandma should be back

any minute."

"Okay"

He makes a few more whines and I take my hand back to try and call his grandmother. She doesn't answer. I try Addison, no answer. My heart beat quickens, and my hands start to shake. Isaac moans again.

"I'll be right back. I promise. Just one second." I rush out of the room and call my mother.

She answers, "Danielle, are you okay?"

"No. I'm here with Isaac by myself and he has to go to the bathroom. He needs help, but I can't do it. I'm so scared. Mom I can't help him. Please can you come over?" I am crying now, and I think my pacing may leave an indentation in the carpet.

"Okay, okay. Calm down. He needs you to be strong. I will be over in a minute."

I hang up the phone and take a deep breath. Trying to gather myself, I grip the phone in one hand and pat it against the other. I stop pacing, shake the fear away, plaster a smile on my face and head back into the room.

"Hey, I don't know when your grandma is coming back but my mom is headed over and then we'll get you taken care of okay?" I smile at him commanding confidence to appear.

"I really have to go!" he cries, the pain in his face increasing.

Self-hate fills me. I can't make myself get him to the bathroom. I don't think I can carry him. What if I drop him? What if he dies and it's just us here? Addison would never forgive me. I'm not strong enough, I'm not good enough. I can't do it and I'm a terrible person.

Suddenly every thought of inadequacy seems to be confirmed as my cowardice harms this poor boy who doesn't deserve an ounce of what he's getting.

I am about to open my mouth again when his grandmother walks in the door. I sigh with relief and rush to her. I take the groceries from her hand as I quickly say, "Isaac needs to go to the bathroom like right now. He needs your help."

She races into the bedroom to help him and I watch her, grocery bags in hand. Addison continues behind me, taking the groceries to the kitchen and I follow. I immediately begin apologizing to her, "I'm so sorry. I couldn't get him to the bathroom. I was freaking out. I'm so sorry."

"It's okay." She continues putting groceries away without so much as a glance at me. She is unphased and numb. I stand still for a second before mimicking her, and we put away the groceries in silence.

When my mother arrives, she and Addison's grandmother talk. I don't know what they say, but I'm sure it isn't pleasant, because when she returns, she takes me home.

. . .

I wake up in the middle of the night to a loud vibrating noise. Addison's name appears and I groggily answer, "Hello?"

"Isaac isn't breathing! He stopped breathing! Please get your mom, come over here right now. Please! There's cop cars and an ambulance-"

"Okay, Okay. Hang tight, I'll be right there".

I'm already half way to my parents' room by the time I hang up. I'm banging on their door, frantically trying to wake up my mother as quickly as I can. My heartrate is pumping loud inside my ears.

"We have to go! Addison wants us over there right now! Isaac isn't breathing!"

She comes out of her room and calmly pulls on her jean jacket, "I just want you to be prepared. This is probably Isaac's last night on Earth."

I nod, and we go out to the car and start driving. My foot bounces in the passenger seat of our Chevy Venture minivan. I glance at the clock every thirty seconds, my foot bouncing faster every time a minute passes and we aren't there. Will he be breathing when we get there?

A right turn onto Addison's street reveals a night sky lit up with red and blue flashes. First responder vehicles line the street, prolonging the time it takes for us to find a place to park. I'm unbuckled before the car has stopped, hand poised on the handle ready to bolt. I spot Addison across the street, hands cupped over her mouth, horror on her face as she stares at her home.

The instant the shifter goes from drive to park, I leap from the car, sprinting to her. I tug her into my embrace, softly "shushing" her pain and stroking her hair. Her head nuzzled in between my shoulder and neck, she lets the tears fall and soak into my shirt. My eyes rest on the front door of her home, waiting. Afraid of what I think I know is true, I squeeze Addison tighter.

Addison spends the next few nights at my house.

The first day after the "incident", we both stay home from school. We lay in my bed with movies playing, but I don't think either of us pays much attention. Our bodies limp and void of emotion, we stay silent as the images flash before us. The day is long and slow moving, allowing plenty of time for my contemplation of life and death.

The second day, my mom tells me I have to go to school. When I leave for the bus, Addison stays home with my mom. I walk from class to class in a haze, fielding questions and remaining silent. Nothing but a bubbling volcano of anguish beneath the surface, by lunch-time I'm doing everything in my power not to cry.

I stare at the food in front of me, replaying it all in my head. I should've gotten the courage to take Isaac to the bathroom. Instead, I let him sit in pain because I was a coward. What kind of person does that? Venom fills my mouth. A girl walks past our table accidentally bumping into me, sending my milk flying and splattering across the white cafeteria floor.

I stare at the chocolate milk puddle growing in front of me and the volcano erupts.

"I can clean it up!" the girl frantically tells me. She thinks I'm crying over spilt milk.

I try to tell her it's not her fault, but my sobs won't let me. I am quivering and the sounds out of my mouth are incoherent. One of my friends at the lunch table comes to my aid. She tells the girl it isn't the milk and wraps her arm around me. The girl goes to get napkins to clean it up anyways.

Meanwhile, my friend holds me and asks, "Are you okay?" The minute the words are out of her mouth my cries become violent and uncontrollable. I cry for Isaac, Addison, my little brother who just lost his best friend. I cry for them, their loss and for how I failed them all. My tears fill her shirt, like Addison's filled mine only a few days before. There seems to be only one sentence I can form.

"It isn't fair."

The Backseat

(16 Years Old)

My knees are crying against the hard tile as I scrub the bathtub. Exertion is radiating from my cheeks, emphasized by the tight ponytail I've pulled my hair into.

"You can't leave this house until you finish cleaning!" my mother reminds me from another room.

"I know!" I yell back as I scrub the tub a little faster, a strand of hair falling out of place.

I don't know if it's the music I'm listening to, the devil's temptation or just my teenage hormones kicking in, but I want to be lip locked with my boyfriend. Right now. I crave the adrenaline and the taste.

"I'm in a mood." I flirtatiously text him.

"A mood?"

"Yeah a mood" I respond with a winking face, trying my hand at being coy.

I fantasize about the events that are about to transpire as I scrub off soap scum. A simple, solid, heavy breathing make out session captures my thoughts. As soon as I finish rinsing the bathtub, I run into my room to change. I smooth my hair over and take a quick look in the mirror before grabbing my keys and heading out the door. The hormones have my foot weighing a little heavier on the gas as I speed down the road and pull into his driveway in record time.

"I'm outside" I text with yet another winking face.

But he is outside and headed toward my driver side door before the text even registers 'sent'. With a mischievous smirk he opens my car door, "Get in the back seat."

I raise an eyebrow at him as I unbuckle and climb into the backseat where he is holding the door open for me.

"Scoot over."

I pull myself over to the opposite side and as soon as I turn my head back to him his lips are on mine. One kiss, two, three and suddenly he's pushing me onto my back. My hands are on the seat trying to hold me up, as I resist a little, but then lean with him.

It doesn't take long for me to feel uncomfortable and I try to sit back up, but he holds me down firm. I open my eyes in shock but continue kissing him. His face is scrunched in persistence. Slowly, I feel his hips make small thrusts as he rubs himself against me. A small objection escapes my lips and I try to reposition myself again. But he moves with me. My body is squirming under his steady grasp. I pray he will pick up on the hint, so I won't have to say anything, but he doesn't. Every time I sit up, I am pushed back down.

My heart sinks, tension builds in my shoulders and suddenly, I can't breathe. I am going weak with fear. Squirming beneath him I am no longer kissing him back, but he presses on. I reposition myself again and again. I am trying to scream, I can't find my voice. He begins to kiss my neck and the fear comes barreling out.

"Stop! Stop! Stop!" I shove him off me with all my might.

He pulls back confused. "I thought- I thought this is what you wanted."

"It's not."

Awkward, uncomfortable and embarrassed I sit up straight and smooth out my shirt. My mind is racing, and my cheeks are hot with chagrin. I think back to the multiple conversations we've had. The ones where I explained my determination to remain abstinent until marriage. Does he think that if he gets me in the right mood, he can just make me change my mind? Is he trying to take advantage of me?

My stomach is doing somersaults and I feel as though I am going to puke. Whatever hormones lead me over here are replaced with fear, anxiety, and panic. A distant memory scratches at the surface of my conscious, but it is foggy and out of reach.

When I pull away from my thoughts and look at him, he's staring at me. My eyes meet his, and he looks at the ground. But avoiding my gaze doesn't hide the angry frustrated breath I hear him push out. His reaction makes me burn hot with rage.

"Get out."

"Wait-" he protests as I push him out of the car and get back in the driver's seat.

"I have to get back home, I told my mom I was only going to be a few minutes."

His tone is sullen as he tells me okay and I pull away faster than I pulled in. Humiliation swallows me whole as I drive home. My hands are still shaking, and I grip the wheel tight to steady them. The color of my knuckles turn from white to blue. My thoughts scream louder than the world and I can't escape them, no matter how loud I blare the radio. Uneven and inconsistent I try to keep my breathing stable to avoid passing out. I barely make it, shaking my head as I turn into my drive way.

The car tires screech, I slam the car door, stride through the house and don't stop when my mother asks me what happened. I throw myself onto my bed and stare at the ceiling.

The scene plays in my head over and over and over. I analyze everything I said, re-reading the text messages searching for the part where I gave him permission to dry hump me.

Tears of frustration begin to fall. What is wrong with me? I desperately search for what's inside, for what's tormenting me. I hunt for the cause of the panic attacks and anxiety ridden outburst. But I come up empty. I let out a small scream, throw my phone across the room and turn out the lights.

Church Camp

(16 Years Old)

It's day four of our five-day summer camp. Which makes it day four of the fight between my heart and head refereed by none other than my anxiety. I can't shake the unsettling feeling my subconscious is hiding something from me. It's not a new feeling, but it's grown in its intensity since arriving here.

The longer we're at camp, the more testimonies I hear, the more frustrated I become. A girl talks about her extreme paranoia that came as a result of being sexually assaulted and I find myself remembering all the times I'd run in fear to seemingly innocent events or people. Another girl talks about her shattered body image, again my soul reaches out, thinking back to the dirty mirror in my bedroom. A small voice inside whispers – me too.

When the testimonies end, I find myself confused at my solidarity with the women. All the symptoms, all the fears, but the cause? I search for a memory in the distance that taunts me. Every time these girls speak, they convey something about my own life, but with a mystery scene my brain has omitted.

I'm frustrated and jumbled as I stand in line for the evening service. I look longingly at the door fifteen feet away, locked until worship begins in thirty minutes. My heart aches for the safety and comfort the music brings. Worship is the place I hear God clearest. The music overtakes my body and transports me someplace else, someplace where it's just me and God. Tonight, I am looking forward to our meeting more than ever.

Finally, the line begins to move, and I make my way down the steep hill into the giant metal building that hosts so many breakthroughs and I pray I will receive mine tonight.

As soon as the pastor leaves the stage to allow the worship team to start, I am running from my seat. I try to get as close to the stage as possible and push my way past a few other people. I need to be close. I need to feel his presence. I need answers.

A long, loud chord fills the silence. Angel-like voices fill the room with praises that reach into my chest and grab my heart. I am singing along as loud as my voice will let me. I sing until I can't sing anymore, and I cry out.

"God! Why do I feel like something happened to me?! What can't I remember?!"

Without warning, I am enveloped by the Holy Spirit. My knees begin to give, and I wobble trying to hold myself up. As if someone has their hands on my shoulders pushing me down, I slam onto the ground. My breaths begin to stagger and like a wave pulling me under, the scene plays before me and I can't escape it. The other people around me vanish, my ears ring until I can't hear the music anymore. Time stands still as memories I had long suppressed rapid fire in front of my eyes, clear as day.

I'm four years old. I'm in bed at my grandparents' house at a sleepover. I lay facing my grandmother's back and my grandfather faces mine. I'm supposed to be asleep. Instead, I'm staring at my grandmother willing her to wake up. I can hear my grandfather breathing heavy in my ear. He reaches his hand around me and under my dress. I flinch at his touch, but only slightly, afraid too much movement might warrant punishment. As he grunts in pleasure, silent tears roll down my baby sized cheeks. I don't dare to speak. I just stare at my grandmother's back as my soul screams out for help and there's no one to answer.

The music returns louder than before as I come out of my trance. Violently, my shoulders shake, and tears pour down onto the floor in front of me. Others around me are jumping and rejoicing, but I am lamenting. The pain rips violently through my throat. So much so, that I think I might lose my voice. My eyes are swollen and feel as though they might pop out of my head.

"No, no. It can't be real. It can't be true." I try to push the memories away, but the memories don't stop, and my childhood begins to make sense. I opened the floodgates and a lifetime of memories demand to be lived. Why I was so uncomfortable with my brothers wrestling. Why my mother playfully smacking my butt sent fear through my body and I screamed at her of its inappropriateness. Why I couldn't watch a sex scene in a movie without crossing my legs at the ghost sensation of being groped. My heart sinks deeper, and I know it's the truth.

Another memory takes over my mind. This time, I'm being instructed to sit on my grandfather's lap in order to take a picture. Every instinct inside me screaming to run, but I try to reassure myself. "He loves you. He's your grandpa. You have too." Everyone in the family staring at me when I hesitate, the pressure to not rock the boat.

As if finally finding that missing piece of the puzzle

I am both relieved to have found the missing piece and horrified to see the final picture. My tears burn hot and a waterfall of emotion flows. I cry through the entire sermon and I cry myself to sleep that night as I mourn the innocence that was robbed from me.

. . .

The entire bus ride home from camp I contemplated how I would tell my mother about my revelation. My life felt as though it was both falling together and falling apart. My odd childhood behavior, paranoia and nightmares were beginning to make sense, but perhaps ignorance was bliss.

When I wake up this morning, I get out of bed in no hurry. The anxiety of my confession gnaws at my stomach. How will she react? How do I tell her? I take my time changing out of my pajamas, brushing my teeth and my hair. Every minute I waste getting ready gives me time to think of what I'll say. When I walk out of my bedroom, my mother is already sitting on the couch. I sit opposite of her and take a deep breath. The words leave my lips slowly, as if begging to stay inside.

"Mom, while I was at camp- I had some things come up." Her eyes fill with a fearful knowing.

She doesn't speak so I continue, "Know how you'd ask me if anything ever happened at grandma and grandpa's? And I'd always say no... well, I always felt like I was lying to you. I always felt guilty, but I couldn't remember anything."

I pause to gauge her reaction. She's holding her breath and I can see the tears threatening to fall. Her pain mimics my own.

"At camp, I had some memories come rushing back to me." My voice starts to catch. "Grandpa molested me."

My mother begins to sob. "I'm so sorry." She repeats to me over and over. "If only I had stopped you from seeing them sooner. But I was still figuring out how to process what they did to me. And they kept calling me crazy. I never meant for you to get hurt. I'm so sorry."

"Mom it's not your fault. You didn't hurt me. Grandpa did. You can't blame yourself."

"I know, but I do." We both cry and sit in a tear-filled silence for a little while before I ask-

"Did you know something had happened to me?"

"I had always guessed. You always acted so strange. But when I took you to a doctor there wasn't any evidence."

I sit there and let her words linger in the air, "How do I tell Dad?"

"Let me do it. I don't know how he will handle it. It's better it comes from me." And with that the conversation is over.

It takes a few days before she works up the courage to tell my father. The morning after she does, he comes down the stairs and gives me this look. I don't know if it was pity, or regret, but it filled me with such sadness and shame. We never spoke of it. Not directly. Any mention of it was pushed off or pushed past. It just became a secret we both knew. How do you talk about a man molesting you to your own father?

I guess you don't.

No More

(16 Years Old)

When I came home from camp, I didn't want to tell anyone about my revelation. My parents were the only ones who knew, and I didn't even really want to tell them.

I hadn't seen a soul outside of my family since returning. I had changed, and I feared everyone would see right through me. I felt strange in my own skin. Skin that didn't feel like my own. Skin that I didn't want to be in. Skin that I scrubbed so roughly in the shower, trying to rid it of the filth I felt, it glowed red with shame. The memory of a man bending my will kept me quiet most days and I locked myself away as often as I could. I had kept silent for such long periods of time, my voice sounded foreign.

But today, my boyfriend was supposed to be coming over to celebrate our six months of dating. It had been arranged before I left for camp and I was dreading it. I didn't leave with us on the best terms, after a miscommunication in the backseat of my car.

Aware of the fact he would be very "hands on" once again, the vomit that threatened to appear in the backseat of my car returned. Barely wanting to be in my own skin I couldn't stand the idea of him touching me. A few hours before he was supposed to come over, I decided to try some open communication and boundaries that my mother was always telling me about.

"Hey, I don't really want to get into it, but can we not be all that physical today? I know we haven't seen each other in a while, but I just don't want to be physical"

"Why?" He responds almost instantly.

"Because. Can you just do that for me, please?"

"But we haven't seen each other in over a week!" His response irritates me immediately and I don't reply.

When he finally gets dropped off at my house, he has a present in his hands. The sight riddles me with guilt. I'm not in the mood to get particularly excited about a present. But I try to act as happy as I can. It's a bracelet. Glowing with pride, he lets me know he saved up a lot of money to buy it. I force a smile and don't tell him that I don't like bracelets. Instead I place it on the counter and give him a fleeting hug.

Our day together feels longer than sitting through a bad movie or the ACTs. And I must tell him at least five or six times to give me some space. His adolescent boy mind seems to have trouble with that request.

"You don't even want to be kissed?!"

It all bothered him. A lot.

We're sitting on the couch and I'm trying to squirm away from his clingy hands when my phone begins to ring. With great relief, I see my best friend's name, Bailey, appear on the screen and I answer it.

"Hey, what's up!"

"I'm standing in line for an open interview! I really think you should come down here. You would be perfect for it."

"Where's it at?"

"It's for Dutch Bros. The interview is in Peoria."

"I've never heard of it? What is it?"

"It's a coffee shop, but it's a drive through and everyone is super bubbly and happy and stuff. Seriously, you'd fit right in!"

"I don't know..." I trail off, not sure that it would really be my scene. Besides, I just got hired at Chick Fil A, a day earlier. But despite my reservations, I can feel the Lord pressing me to obey. "I'll think about it a minute and call you back."

I say good bye and I turn to my boyfriend who is fuming.

"You already have a job!"

"I know, but I just have this feeling like I'm supposed to go to this thing!"

"We haven't seen each other in a week, you won't let me touch you, and it's our six months!"

"We've spent all day together, I told you I needed space – which you said was fine – and I really feel like God is telling me to go to this interview."

"Why would God tell you to go to an interview if you already have a job?!"

"I don't know. But I am going. So, either get your stuff and I'll take you home or you can walk."

Frustrated with each other we climb into my Saturn station wagon in silence. We don't say a single word the entire drive to his house. In fact, as soon as I bring the car to a halt in front of his yard, he gets out, slams the door and proceeds to walk towards his house without so much as a glance at me. I'm irate and can't roll my window down fast enough.

"Really? That's how you want today to end? You're really mad because I'm going to an interview, I feel like God wants me to go to?"

"You didn't hardly pay any attention to me! You wouldn't even touch me!"

Our words get meaner as our argument gets hotter. He couldn't understand why I would do this, and I couldn't understand why he couldn't understand my point of view. He turns, yells and begins pacing in his driveway. I stare at him in disbelief at his unwillingness to cooperate with me. In his rage, he punches his mother's car. My jaw hangs open. When I recover, I throw my hands up in the air.

"That's it. I'm leaving."

I can't believe he would resort to physical violence and I decide that is all I need to know about a possible future with him. I hear him scream my name as I drive down the street and he realizes his mistake.

As I drive off, my phone begins buzzing and it doesn't stop. Ten minutes into my drive I have to turn my phone off because he is relentless and it is so distracting.

When I get to the interview, I turn my phone back on to several missed calls and messages. I shake my head, put it in my back pocket and walk over to where I see Bailey.

I begin to tell her everything, but I'm so flustered the words keep getting tangled in my mouth. My mind and emotions are racing. I huff out a forceful breath.

"I just don't know who he thinks he is!"

"He's an idiot", she tells me like any good friend would. "Just focus on this interview."

I follow her advice and welcome the distraction with open arms. Looking around there are people of all walks of life and apparently all kinds of closets. I see girls in cute dresses and some in booty shorts and spaghetti strap undershirts. There are men in polos and cargo shorts, while others wear white tank tops and cutoff jeans.

We wait in line for almost an hour and a half before it's our turn to interview. Even with plenty of time to lighten up it takes all my will power to seem pleasant and well put together. I answer honestly with thin veils of pep, because I don't have the energy to give an "interview-ready" version. At one point, they ask me what color I would be if I was a color and why.

"Pink, because I'm bright and bubbly and pink is a

pretty happy color" I say in complete irony to how I am actually feeling. Also, despite the fact I hate the color pink.

Thankfully, the interviews only last a few minutes. Once we are finished, I get Bailey to convince her mom to let her stay the night at my house. I need the distraction and she's the only one for the job.

Early the next morning, we explain it all to my mother. My boyfriend, for however long I would still call him that, obviously was up early as well, because his attempts to reach out to me started only a few minutes into my mother's debriefing. Every other sentence is accompanied by a vibration that radiates through the kitchen counter. I try my best to ignore it, but I don't last long. Aggressively, I reach for the phone and respond to his fifty messages.

"I don't want to talk to you" I type so forcefully it hurts my thumbs.

My phone stops vibrating, and I sigh in relief, but he simply changes his target. Bailey's phone rings and she answers.

"Are we at the house?" she repeats his question as if not correctly hearing him.

My eyes widen in horror and I shake my head violently swiftly moving my hand across my neck to signify as boldly as possible to deny the truth.

"No, we're out shopping." She covers elegantly, my beautiful deceitful best friend always to my rescue.

They hang up and I thank her. "He'll show up here if he thinks we're home."

She nods but says, "He called us liars."

My heart sinks and not three minutes later there is a knock at the front door. Like a deer in headlights I don't move. My mother looks at the door and then back at me.

"DO NOT ANSWER IT!" I whisper yell, "Mom, please. We are not home."

"You have to deal with this Danielle. Just do it now." With that, in her typical bold fashion, she heads to the door.

"Mom do NOT let him in. I will deal with it, just not now."

I pray that she listens to me as she leaves to answer the door. But when I hear his voice followed by my mother's warm welcome, I panic.

Hurriedly, I grab Bailey's hand and pull her into the

walk-in pantry and shut the door softly. I turn around and look at her in disbelief of my own actions.

"What are we doing?" her eyebrows raise, and I have no good answer. Her facial expression is barely readable in the dark tiny room, but I see the concern in it. I've lost my mind.

"I don't know. My mom let him in, I panicked! I don't know."

We stare at each other waiting for the other one to make a move. More than anything I just want to disappear from existence. I press my ear to the door, and I don't hear any voices, but some glassware clings in the cabinet nearest the pantry that we are currently hiding in. I assume it's my mother getting something to drink for her unwelcomed house guest.

As quietly and slowly as I can manage, I push the door open just enough to see out with one eyeball. Hoping to see my mother, I am met with a very agitated boyfriend getting a water glass out of the cabinet. His mouth is pulled into a straight line and he continues to pull the glass out all while maintaining eye contact with me. I shut the door again and look at Bailey.

"He saw me."

"Now what?"

"If we stay in here, do you think he'll take the hint and leave?"

Bailey frowns and I know it's time to face the excruciatingly embarrassing music. My inescapable boyfriend stares at me in contempt as I exit the pantry and walk over to the kitchen table. I fight the urge to stare at the ground and curl up into the pathetic ball I feel like. Instead, I hold my head high and try to make my strides look elegant.

For a moment we don't speak. I wait for anyone else to break the tension. I look at him, then at Bailey and finally my mother, who shoots me a look of disappointment and expectation. We sit a minute more, looking from one another in awkward silence. Another scowl from my mother prompts me to take a deep breath and look back at the angry boy across the kitchen.

"Hey, let's go in the other room and talk." I walk towards him and hold my hand out in front of me, gesturing him to walk into the other room.

We leave Bailey and my mom at the kitchen table and head to the formal sitting room. But when we get there, I don't sit. I am filled with embarrassment, shame, fear and I need this to be over. I need it to end now.

"I don't think this is going to work out."

"What why!?" He's in disbelief and I'm shocked that he didn't see it coming.

"It just isn't."

I don't want to explain how he terrifies me. I don't want to admit to my trauma or confront him about the fist he threw and how I'm afraid he might be capable of hitting me. I just want him out of my house.

"We just had that really nice day together before the fight and I bought you that really expensive gift-" He tries to barter more time.

I scoff. I can't believe he is using the fact he bought me something as a reason for why I shouldn't break up with him. Or that he considered yesterday a "nice time". I hold up my hand and stop him in his tracks.

"Fine. I'll go get it."

I storm out of the room and retrieve the gift that he was now using as a bargaining chip. When I return, he is sitting on the couch. I forcefully thrust my hand at him, holding the gift out for him to take. "Here."

"No, I'm not going to take it." He leans back into

the couch, crosses his arms and challenges me with his expression. Maintaining eye contact, I place the gift on the table in front of him. I am done playing games.

"Let me get the rest of it." I storm off again. But just as I turn the corner with various items in tow, I see him slip out the front door and slam it shut. I look down at the floor and there is the bracelet, right next to the door, where he clearly left it to make a statement.

I open the door and yell, "You forgot your stupid bracelet!"

He doesn't turn around and I don't chase him. I don't care if he left the stupid bracelet. I don't care that he walked 10 miles to see me, when I specifically told him not to come. I don't care about the rumors he will spread. I don't care. Because I am done feeling unsafe and paranoid for the sake of his ego.

An Affair to Remember

(16 Years Old)

My comforter holds me as the melody from my earbuds soothes my soul. I take note of the small imperfections in the drywall of my ceiling. The white paint almost makes them undetectable, but I've been staring at them for hours and after the first few, they begin to come out of hiding.

I've taken to sulking in my room like this since the strangeness began. Everyone is walking on eggshells. The tension like a vacuum, sucking the joy out of doing anything else. Something is going on. There's a secret my parents won't share. They have entrusted me with family secrets as serious as murder, yet here we sit and I "can't be told". Being kept in the dark is like an itch I can't scratch. It bothers me to my core. How can I be raised with brutal honesty and then treated like a child at the age of sixteen?

I attempt to dissect the mystery by trying to imagine what my father's friends could've done to offend my mother so badly that she has forced me to unfriend them on Facebook. When I objected, she only had this to say:

"Know when you tell a child not to chase after a ball that's rolled into the street? The child doesn't understand why, but you know it's to keep them safe. You're the child and I'm telling you not to chase the ball."

Her weird analogy made me uncomfortable, but I complied. If not only out of frustration. My mental investigation is interrupted by a knock on the door. I take out my earbuds and call for the knocker to enter.

"Hey sweetheart." My father cracks open the door and sticks his head in, "How are you?"

"I'm fine. Frustrated that you and mom won't tell me what's going on but I'm fine."

"Yeah, look." He steps into my room, coming to sit on the bed beside me. "Your mother really doesn't want you to know. But I know that you're like me. And you'd rather know something bad and work through it than just wonder and drive yourself crazy. And I know you're old enough and mature enough to handle the truth."

My heart lifts as I realize he's about to share with me what my mother's been hiding. But as quickly as it rises, it falls. I see his eyes begin to pool with tears threatening to shed.

"You know I love your mother. And I love you-" I wait for the inevitable "but" and sure enough it comes.

He continues to share about a relationship he had begun developing with a woman he works with. The excuses roll off his tongue quicker than I can digest them. "When your mother was working through her trauma, I just felt so alone. I never knew who I would be coming home too. Somedays she wanted me around, other days I wasn't even allowed to touch her. I guess I just started to distance myself emotionally. It was nothing physical - me and this woman. It was strictly emotional. We just...connected."

I match his tears with my own, but mine are made with anger. My heart hardens. "I'm so sorry!" He apologizes profusely. "I hate that I hurt your mother, but I hate that I hurt you kids even more."

"So, is that what I should expect when I get married?! That whoever I marry is just going to cheat and that's just the way it is?!" I hiss through clenched teeth.

Hot boiling rage fills me at the realization of his words. Her trauma is his excuse. The words feel personal. Will my trauma be another man's excuse one day?

"No, no, no. What I did was wrong, and I am so

very sorry. I am trying to make it right."

"Is that why mom made me unfriend Jesse and Aaron on Facebook?" I begin to put the pieces together.

"There was a picture... We went bowling and the woman had her head on my lap. Jesse and Aaron were in the picture. Your mom thinks they knew about it and were hiding it from her. But they weren't! They had no idea."

Time stretches, and I become more lost by the minute. My heart turned to ice, cracks and crumbles and I ask to be alone. He tells me he loves me and apologizes once again before leaving the room.

I don't move from my bed; I just sit staring at my hands in disbelief. I want to scream. I want to run away. Both behaviors, I've always curbed when upset, but this time I'm done being the good girl who takes her punches sitting down. Jumping out of bed and slipping on my shoes, I grab my keys. My father is sitting in the living room watching tv when I walk by.

"Where are you going?"

"Driving."

I don't tell him where I am going because I don't know. I have nowhere to run or hide, but I can't be home. I need to be alone, away from the problem, away from the pain.

When I start driving and realize that I don't have any place to go, I turn around and drive to the White Tank mountains. It's almost thirty minutes away, but I don't care.

My hands grip the steering wheel so tight I think my hands might permanently lose their color. I drive away from the happy suburbs and towards nothingness. I roll down the windows, driving quickly down an empty street allowing the pain to rip through me in a scream. I slow down only to pull up to the toll booth, pay the admission fee and drive halfway up a mountain. The road winds in every direction. Only one car passes me since the park will be closing soon. The emptiness greets me like a warm fire in the winter. I want the world to myself, even if just for a moment.

I don't stop driving until I find a small cliff that overlooks the surrounding towns and terrain below. It's to the left of me and is about three times the size of a highway shoulder. It's just big enough to fit one, maybe two cars. It seems sturdy enough and I'm tired of driving. So, I turn onto it. I slowly creep my car as close to the edge as I dare to go, cut the engine and look down at the landscape below.

Most people don't think Arizona is beautiful. Before, I had never considered it anything other than bland. Some dirt, mostly brown with some cacti and dark green or brown half dead bushes. It was a desert, nothing special. But in this moment, it is the most beautiful, serene place I could be.

I turn up my radio loud enough that I can't hear my thoughts, watch the sky darken as night grows closer and allow *Cigarette Daydreams* by Cage the Elephant to wash over me and take away the pain. I analyze the horizon and dream that I never have to go back. Out here there are no love affairs, no taunting trauma filled memories, no evil family members, no worries. Out here, I am free.

The song ends, and I let a few more go by before I decide to turn over the engine and start back home. I can't hide forever because that would make me a coward, but more importantly because I have two little brothers at home who don't know what is going on. Suddenly my mission is clear. I must protect them. My parents have the emotional stability of 16-year-olds at the moment, how can they be trusted to watch out for my brother's best interest? It always comes to this: if I can save them, I will.

My phone rings and a picture of my father appears.

"Where are you?"

"I'm at the White Tanks. I'm driving home now. I'll be home soon. I just needed time alone."

While I am livid with my father and there's a hole in my heart. I can't help but still appreciate the fact that even in a time like this he understands. My mother would've never let me leave the house. She would've forced me to stay and talk to her. The exact opposite of what I needed.

My father seriously messed up, I'm fuming at the circumstance he has created, but I try to understand. Mostly because I don't want to believe my father is a bad guy. But also, I was there. Despite her unconditional love, my mother could be a roller coaster of emotion and "new versions" of herself. But she always tried her best and she doesn't deserve what my father did. I'm pulled in so many directions, an outpour of feelings wash over me. Tears well and a shaky breath escapes my lips. Tired of crying, I shut my brain off and just drive.

When I get home, I don't talk to my father. I walk past the tv and straight into my bedroom. He doesn't say anything and neither do I. Instead, I lay back down where

I was before and act like nothing ever happened.

At the Altar

(17 Years Old)

I'm on my knees, head bowed, legs touching my chest as I try to get as low to the ground as I feel. My back is heaving heavily and I'm sure my sobs are louder than the worship band. I've lost control.

I can feel the congregation looking at me, the only one up at the altar during worship. Every. Single. Time. My throat is raw, my eyes are swollen, and my face is stained with tear streaks. I've stopped wearing makeup to church for this reason.

"WHY?! Why God. Why would you let me go through that? I was a child! 4 years old! How could you let me suffer like this? It affected my whole life!"

I'm yelling at God in my head. No one else can hear, but I am sure it is ringing in his ears. "It's the reason I'm always looking over my shoulder. Why I cringe at seemingly innocent things. My anxiety! How could you?" I stop my sobbing long enough to catch a breath. I look up to the ceiling, defeated and torn, "Why didn't you protect me?"

My sobs are growing weaker. I've cried so much, I'm beginning to run out of tears. I am exhausted in every sense of the word.

The band changes songs, the loud hope-filled tune fades out and is replaced with a much softer one. As the lead singer, quiet and skillful in his art, carefully sings a song of redemption, a peace begins to wash over me. My tears are quieted and like a soft whisper inside my heart, echoing in my thoughts, I hear his voice. The one whom I just cursed, rushes to comfort me.

"My daughter. I love you greatly. I am so sorry this happened and that you have to fight this battle. But I promise, it will all be for good. You will have strength greater than you've ever known. My dear, your pain will not be for nothing."

Slowly, I let the words sink in. I use them to bandage the wounds, stand up for the first time in weeks and join the band in praise.

"There may be pain in the night, but joy comes in the morning."

Sh- Hit the Fan

(17 Years Old)

The table is quiet. The tension palpable. If I wanted, I could probably reach out, scoop it up and place it on my plate next to the tasteless dinner my mother has made. The dinner really isn't bad, but it lacks the love it's usually made with. Instead, its coated in obligation and anger. I have to swallow hard to make the food go down and to keep my mind from wandering towards the silence. Finally, my mother speaks up.

"John, why don't you tell them what happened."

"Beth..." he trails off.

My brothers look at each other. I look at them and then back at my parents. Everything inside me protests. I've known about the betrayal, the fights, the secrets, but my brothers have been left out of it this far. My eyes are wide at my mother's request. They're 14 and 12. They don't need to know. Why is she doing this?

My mother's voice raises, grows in passion as she barks, "Tell them or I will!"

Despite her threat, my father doesn't speak.

Shame fills his eyes and he looks down. He's searching for the words. He starts a sentence and then re-starts. He's too slow for my mother. She begins yelling about the mistress whose husband found them in the backseat of a car. My father quickly tries to explain it away. They were just talking. It wasn't physical.

"Why would you need to be in the back seat to talk?! You're lying. Why would her husband beat your truck and lay his hands on you?!"

"Stop!" My father begs for mercy.

Suddenly I'm fading away. My brothers and I aren't apart of the conversation anymore. My mother is standing and screaming. Their fight is growing bigger, louder, hotter, when Joe grabs his plate and calmly rinses it off in the sink. Luke, our youngest brother, follows. And finally, myself.

My parents have stopped arguing long enough to see we've all left the table. They're quietly staring at me and Luke who are staring at them. Joe has retreated to his bedroom upstairs. Not one for confrontation, I'm not surprised that he's the first one to leave. Deciding to follow his lead, I grab my keys from the kitchen counter.

"I'm taking the boys, I will bring them back later.

But this is not something they need to see." I turn to Luke and tell him to go get Joe.

"Where are you going to go?" My mother asks, frustrated.

My anger boils at their lack of control. At my mother's tactic of using her children to further shame her husband. Not caring about the impact, it will have on my brothers lives. How my father can't find any words, despite having ample time to have thought of what he might have said if it all came out. For still seeing the woman, when he told me it was done.

"I don't know." I curtly respond.

I hear my brothers' footsteps and I grab my purse and leave. As I shut the front door, I think I hear them begin to argue again.

We get in the car and I start driving. I don't know where I'm going. I'm not even focused on the road. All my energy is being directed towards holding the tears at bay. I plead my emotions to stop, begging for strength. I don't want my brothers to see me cry. I glance in the rearview mirror. Both their eyes are fixated on the floor. The sight pushes me over the edge, and I focus on trying to see through the betrayal of my tears. None of us speak.

Before I know it, I've pulled into the parking lot of Dutch Bros. The only place I have felt family, love and support for the last year. I know now there's a reason God made me go to that open interview long ago. He knew I would need this support.

I tell my brothers to walk up to the front window and order whatever they want, and promise to be back in a few minutes. I run to the back door and walk into the tiny coffee shack.

I scan the shack for who's working, praying it's someone who will understand. As soon as my eyes meet Dillon's, I quickly walk to the only corner invisible from the outside. He finishes up what he's doing and comes to find me. In between violent sobs, I explain everything. The secrets, the pain, the fights, and now tonight's hell show.

Dillon and my other coworker, Austin, take turns comforting and encouraging me. "You're handling this all with such grace." "You did the right thing." I let their words soak into my soul and soothe the wounds.

After what feels like hours, I hug them for the sixteenth time, splash water on my face and walk out front. My brothers are sitting at the patio table furthest from the window. They don't talk to each other, just stare at their phones. I look to see what they ordered and notice they only have the water I told Austin to give them.

"You sure you guys don't want something else? You can get whatever you want."

They don't look up. "No, it's fine."

I text my best friend Bailey. "Hey shit hit the fan. I'm coming over with my brothers".

She responds quickly and when we get to her house, she doesn't ask for an explanation, just opens the door and puts on a movie to help distract us.

The dialogue is nothing but noise. My thoughts are far away. I am suddenly aware that nothing is going to be the same. I am the only one protecting them. Wedged between my brothers on Bailey's couch I put my arms around them, despite being much, much shorter than them both. My heart breaks for the end of my parents' marriage, but it breaks even more for my brothers. All I've ever wanted in this life was to keep them safe. Protect them as much as I could. Yet again, I feel like a failure.

My phone buzzes and lights up with a message

from my mother, "Where are you?"

"We're watching a movie." I vaguely respond.

I don't want her to know where we are. I clench my teeth so hard it hurts. She doesn't deserve to know. The way she willingly hurt my brothers. The way she didn't even try to protect them. I'm filled with disgust and turn off my phone when she tries to call.

We will come home when my brothers are ready, I say to myself. But truly I don't want to go home. If I could, I would stay out all night. I let a few more minutes go by. If only I was older, with more money, enough to get a place and kidnap my brothers.

Joe sees the turmoil I must have written on my face and hugs me, trying to offer comfort. I look at him and smile, but he shouldn't feel the need to comfort me. I'm the big sister. I'm the one who was supposed to protect them. Confusion on how we got here and pain I couldn't stop it beg for my attention. I focus back on the movie and briefly consider asking to stay the night. But avoidance is not a trait I want to teach my brothers. So, we thank Bailey for the refuge and head home to face whatever horrors await.

Locked and Loaded

(17 Years Old)

As I round the corner headed into the loft, I catch a glimpse of my father making the bed in the spare bedroom. He's been sleeping there for the past week or so. My mother has kicked him out of her bedroom.

I noticed they bickered a lot before, but it's been a verbal wrestling match between the two for the last month. It's finally all out in the open, the secret I had been keeping for almost a year- my father cheated.

Ironically enough, my mother has decided the best response is to date some other man herself. "I'm in love with him." She told us. The statement didn't seem sincere, but it took me by surprise anyway. Since then, they've spent a lot of time in their respective rooms.

I check on my brothers before I head to school. "You guys all ready?"

"Yup" they respond, backpacks poised and ready to go. It's almost eerie how normal we all try to behave while our parents' marriage crumbles right in front of us. We don't show much emotion. My brothers and I seem to be playing a game of who can act the most unbothered. Luke is winning.

"Alright, have a good day. I love you."

When I come back home late that night after school and a full 6-hour shift at the coffee shop, I notice something is off.

My mother is standing at the top of the stairs, just staring down at me as I walk in the front door. I look up at her and when she doesn't say anything, I begin to climb the stairs. The silence calls me. Not just her silence, but the house. I don't hear my brother's videogames or their laughter. My father is nowhere to be seen and my stomach is in knots.

"What's going on? Where's Dad?"

"Danielle, your father isn't coming home anymore."

"What? Why?" I say annoyed.

"Well, we were fighting, and he grabbed the gun from our bedroom and ran into the guest bedroom and locked the door. When I ran after him and started banging on the door, he wouldn't answer. I called the police, I was afraid he might hurt himself." She says it all so matter-of-fact. Her words, ghost of emotion, flow through me.

My mind jumps all over, the story sounds made up. There's no way my father would do that. Would he? I try to think of any warning signs I would've seen then - "Where are Joe and Luke? Did they see it all?"

My heart drops at the idea of them having to witness the police dragging my father out of his own home.

She looks down. "They were here. They're in my bedroom watching a movie."

I sigh deeply, "Jesus, Mom. You really think Dad was going to hurt himself?"

She tries to say she heard him clicking the gun into place, but I choose not to believe it. It sounds too much like a soap opera. I push past her and head to where my brothers try to numb the pain with the distraction of yet another movie. Our family's choice drug to numb our brains from the real pain. We leave this world for another, if only for an hour and a half.

I knock on the door and gently open it, "Hey, are you guys okay?"

They shrug and keep watching the movie. Unsure of what I could say to fix anything, I just tell them to let me know if they need anything and head down the stairs to my room.

I drop my bag on the floor, shut my door and climb under the covers. Like opening a cage of lions, I let my mind run wild. I'm angry and I'm irritated I wasn't here to stop it. Instead, I was at work. I was laughing with coworkers, making large frappes and small hot coffees. And my brothers were here, alone.

I toss and turn in my bed, unable to get comfortable. My jeans are scratchy against my skin, but I refuse to take them off. The act of stubbornness hurts only myself. It's pointless, but still, I leave them on. Tears of frustration slide down my red cheeks as I take inventory of all the bad breaks I've been having. I recount church camp revelations and parental brawls. I wallow in the self-pity until I drift into sleep, my only relief.

Apartment 205

(17 Years old)

I'm briefly lifted out of my seat as I drive over a speed bump a little too fast. I apologize to my brothers for the bumpy ride as they groan at the abrupt shake. We're driving to my father's new apartment. It's only a few minutes away from the house we grew up in. 10 years of seemingly perfect suburban happiness in that house. Look where we are now.

The plan is that we spend the weekend at his new place and then every other weekend after this. I haven't seen him in several days and it feels like I'm driving to meet him for the first time, like he's a stranger. I ask my brothers if they feel nervous, but I know we all are. The last time we saw our dad he had been taken away by the police for being a "danger to himself". I wasn't there. I don't know if I believe it. But it makes me uneasy anyways.

I pull into the apartment complex and realize I have no idea where his apartment is or what section of the complex we should be parking in. I pick up my phone and hit my father's speed dial.

"Hey. We're here, but I don't know where to park."

"Just park somewhere and I'll come find you."

I park right where I'm at. As the boys and I gather our things and get out of the car, I see my dad headed our way. He's all smiles, as he says, "You parked right by my apartment, what are the chances?" His feeble attempt at a joke forces me to crack an awkward smile and give him a hug.

We follow him to apartment 205, on the second floor. After a tour of the small two-bedroom, one bath floorplan, my brothers sit on the couch and my dad pulls me into the tiny apartment kitchen to help him make a frozen pizza.

"What do you think of the place?"

"It's nice. Really cute – I always liked apartments better than houses anyways. There's less to clean."

He smiles at my attempt to make him feel better. I know he's the one who cheated in the first place, but I feel sorry for him anyways. "I'm really sorry I don't have anything better to eat."

"The boys love frozen pizza. They're in heaven. Don't worry about it, Dad."

"Do you want to go get the mail with me?"

I nod, and we leave the boys to watch a movie while my father and I walk across the apartment complex to the mailboxes.

"How's your mom? Is she doing okay?" His question feels like a stab to the heart.

I try to give an honest answer without going into too much detail. I feel weird telling him about my mother when I know she holds nothing but anger and bitterness towards him. She's right to be angry, but I wish she'd be less obvious about it. Thankfully, we make it to the mailbox, before he can ask me for any details.

We grab the mail and are back up the stairs at his door. He reaches for the door knob, but falters. I see his shoulders slump and his will shatter.

"It's just been so hard." He turns back around and looks at me, tears in his eyes, "I am so sorry I don't have more to offer. I really didn't mean to hurt you guys."

My father begins sobbing, he takes a step towards me and I meet him with an embrace. My eyes are wide as I stare at the door that separates us from my brothers. His tears soak my shirt and I tell him everything will be alright.

[107]

"Look, I wanted it to work out for you guys, but right now it doesn't look that way. And I'm really sorry, but you need to just start looking at this next chapter in your life." He nods and gathers himself. My own tears threaten to escape, but I hold firm.

"The boys are right on the other side of that door – you have to pull yourself together. Look, you and mom, you've never hid anything from me and that's fine. But those boys still see you guys as parents. So, you have to suck it up for them. It's going to be alright. Your life isn't over. It's just changing."

I'm sad and angry all at the same time, "You've always been so mature. I don't know how you turned out so good." My dad looks at me with admiration. I shift uncomfortably at the odd feeling of being my father's counselor.

"Me either, but hey let's be glad I did." I joke with him, desperate at this point to get us inside to my brothers. But before we do, I must ask one question.

"Dad, why did you take the gun and lock yourself in your room?"

"Why? What does your mom say?"

"She says you were going to hurt yourself."

He laughs sarcastically. "I wasn't going to hurt myself. We were arguing, and she was getting very emotional and I didn't want her to have it. I thought it would be safer with me in my room."

I stare at him suspiciously. He takes a breath and pauses just a moment before pressing on.

"Do you think you'd be okay if I started dating? Your mother has moved on, she makes it very clear. I don't think I can keep holding out hope for us anymore."

I think about it for a moment, completely unprepared for a question like that to follow the moment we just had.

"I think that's only fair. As long as it isn't her."

I don't know her name, the woman my father cheated with, and I don't want too. But the idea of my father ending up with the women who broke his marriage in the first place seems like the worst possible ending to this mess.

He looks at me, searching for something, but responds with "Okay." And the conversation is over.

We both take a deep breath and prepare ourselves to enter this new chapter as we walk into the living room of apartment 205.

Round Three

(17 Years Old)

The kitchen table's wooden chair is cold as I wiggle into it for yet another family meeting. I'm beginning to despise the term, along with this high-top table that has been the arena for so much drama already. In front of me stands both of my parents, which makes me raise an eyebrow, but only for a second before I realize what's happening.

"Your father is going to move back in."

"Are you guys getting back together?" Joe asks.

"We're going to try to work it out." My mother replies.

"Are you going to sleep in the same room again?" I ask out loud, the question surprisingly bold and provocative for how quickly I'm wanting this to be over.

"We're going to start out in different rooms. There is some trust that needs to be regained" My mother answers and I silently scoff.

There are a few beats of silence as they wait for us

to ask more questions and we wait for further explanation.

"Can we go now?" I break the silence, impatient and intolerant of their ideas.

"Yeah, you can go."

I can feel myself sizing them up, looking for the holes in their plan. It wasn't very long ago my mother was at my father's throat. The sudden shift makes me uneasy.

If I can only be thankful for one part of this mess, it's that it has allowed me privacy and distraction. I spend the quiet time in my room researching trauma and counseling strategies and principles.

I begin applying them to myself in any way possible. I work on managing my emotions and confronting the trauma exposed this past summer, trying to find closure.

My parents might be a mess and sure, they've forgotten my revelation of abuse, but at least they're leaving me alone. If they want to get back together, fine. If they want to break up, fine. I need to deal with the fact that at work the other day I dropped to the ground in fear when a coworker playfully grabbed me from behind.

I can't focus on my parent's anymore. If I'm not careful, I'm going to fall apart with them.

A Peace Offering

(17 Years Old)

My mother knocks on the door frame of my open door. I'm sitting on my bed reading a book. My new favorite escape. Sleeping had started to give me headaches and I'd slept so much I couldn't sleep anymore. So now in order to leave this world behind I enter into fantasy worlds by the way of literature.

"Hey, would you want a bunny?"

"A bunny?"

"Yeah, like as an early birthday present. I thought you might like a bunny."

"Uh, sure."

"Awesome, let's go shopping for a cage, what do you think?"

"Okay." I am cautious at the sudden friendly arrangement, but the idea of a cute furry creature doesn't sound bad, so we climb in the car and go looking for his new home.

. . .

Every store we've looked at hasn't had anything nearly big enough to be comfortable for a bunny. We're still looking, but we've had to travel almost an hour and a half away from home. I don't even recognize the part of Phoenix that we're in.

We enter a Home Depot as our last resort to maybe make something ourselves before giving up for the night. We're walking down the length of the store peering into each aisle when suddenly we both stop. The profile of an older man looking at a small metal part catches our attention.

It's my grandfather.

As soon as I recognize and register the man down the aisle as my grandfather, the man whose bed I was forced to sleep in, whose lap I was forced to sit in and whose kisses I was forced to accept, fear shoots up my spine and down my legs. I see the man's profile begin to turn and I run.

I leave my mother behind without so much as a word and bolt for the other end of the store. I make it about seven aisles before my asthma stops me and I quickly turn into the aisle immediately to my right. Bent over, hands on my knees, breathing heavy I wait for my mother to catch up.

I look up at my mother as she comes around the corner quietly saying my name.

"Danielle! Danielle? What are you doing?"

"I'm sorry, I just can't. I don't know. I just ran."

Her expression is soft. "You should go talk to him."

My eyes grow twice their size and I almost audibly gasp. "TALK TO HIM? What are you crazy?"

"Danielle, you can't spend your life running away. He's an old man now. He can't hurt you. You could easily over power him. You just need to confront your fears."

"No. No way. Are you going to talk to him?"

"I don't want to, but I'm not the one running away. I'm not afraid of him anymore."

I just stand there. My hands are still resting on my knees. My mouth still agape.

"No. I am not going to talk to him."

"Alright, fine. Let's go see if we can find a bunny cage."

Every time we go down a new aisle, I am slow to look down it, trying to avoid a run in with my grandfather. I try to act normal whenever my mother shoots me side glances, but I still look as helpless and scared as I feel.

After assessing the aisles for bunny cage making materials, we come up empty handed. I am hopeful that my grandfather is long gone when we exit the store and head towards my mother's minivan. But as soon as we walk into the street, sure enough my grandfather has just gotten to his truck. My mother looks at me.

"Are you sure you don't want to say anything to him?" Her eyes challenge me, and I know she will be disappointed if I say no. I stay silent looking between her and him.

Afraid to say yes, but unable to say no, my mother makes up her mind and begins walking towards him.

"Mom, mom. Stop." I beg. She pretends to not hear me as her course has already been set.

She leads the way over as she calls out to him, "Hi Dad."

"Bethy! Danielle! Wow you look so grown up, you're so beautiful." He reaches out to hug me and I freeze.

My skin screams in protest, but fear makes me hug him back. Still afraid of being reprimanded for disobedience.

"What are you doing here?" he asks.

My mom looks at me, but I stay quiet. I refuse to say a word. "We're looking for a cage. Danielle is going to get a bunny as an early birthday present."

"Yeah, but we didn't find one, so we're headed home now." I say pointedly.

"Well, don't leave yet. Let me call your grandmother. She will kill me if I don't call her and have her come up here. She's been dying to see you Danielle. She talks about you all the time." The way he says it almost makes me feel guilty.

"I don't know..." I start, but he cuts me off.

"It will only take a moment. We don't live far." With that he walks away to talk to my grandmother on the phone. "She'll be here in just a few minutes."

I just stare at my mother, feeling like that same 4-year-old girl again. Helpless.

"So, what's been going on?" He looks at us both, expectantly.

I look around, anywhere but him. I shift from foot to foot, uncomfortable and anxious. I can tell he is much frailer. He spent his life as a Farrier and it shows. His body is broken, and his walk has become more of a hobble. He looks nothing like the man I remember from 10 years ago. Still, it doesn't make me feel any better.

Finally, my grandmother shows up and she is almost out of the car before it's fully parked. She comes straight to me and wraps me in a big hug. "Doodlebug, I missed you!"

She looks at my mom and gives her a curt hug, but quickly turns her focus back to me. She is swift to ride down memory lane asking me if I remember various occasions from when I was little. Sticking my tongue out when I used to draw. Trying to get secret rides on her electric scooter by simply saying "vroom vroom" to keep my brothers in the dark. I nod along to it all, of course I remember. I side eye my mother silently begging her to get me out of here.

When my mother comes to my rescue and says we have to go, my grandfather gives me another hug which I side step and turn into a side hug. All too aware of every inch of his body.

My grandmother embraces me next and whispers in my ear. "I never stopped thinking about you. Tell your mom to let you see me. I tried, but she doesn't listen. I will always love you. Remember when you said that to me? I love you so much doodlebug."

"I love you too."

I say it simply because I can't bear the thought of any confrontation. I would probably say anything to be able to leave at this moment. So, I smile as I say goodbye and climb into the car.

It's odd to see them, looking so normal. I laugh to myself. It's all so ridiculous. We looked like a normal family in that parking lot. No one would ever have guessed those two old people had threaten to bake my mother. They've committed unspeakable crimes. Things I can't even iterate or write. And there we were just "catching up".

We are on the highway headed back to our house when my mother speaks up. "Are you glad we talked to them?"

I'm quiet for a moment, still stuck in thought. I chew on my mother's question and respond, "Maybe you were right. It was at least good for closure."

A strange calm washes over me. I didn't tell them off or demand answers. I even lied and still played the role of the perfect granddaughter. But I'm an adult now. Today, I got to walk away of my own free will. His control over me seems to weaken. The monster from my memory, no longer so scary.

The Transition

(18 Years Old)

I'm standing at the dinner table with my laptop in front of me and college invitation letters spread out. I am going through them one by one, comparing prices and programs, when I notice my father across the table, sizing me up.

"Do you have something you want to say?" I ask, daring him to speak.

"No." He lightheartedly replies. His shoulders do a slight shrug of indifference.

I go back to my work as I pull up the website for Arizona State University. Although extremely expensive, it's my top pick. I say a silent little prayer that I scored high enough on my ACT to get a full ride.

"Have you ever considered applying for a college out of state?" My father levies.

I keep my head down, but look up at him with a raised eyebrow, "No, out of state tuition is ridiculous. Besides, where would I even go?"

"You might get scholarships. I was looking and

there seems to be some good ones in Missouri."

My eyes narrow on him. His motive for prompting the question comes clearer into view. I hadn't heard of Missouri outside of a 5th grade geography lesson. Why on Earth would he suggest spending an even more absurd amount of money to go to college in the middle of nowhere?

"Dad are we moving to Missouri?" I cut to the chase, tired of the games my family has been playing.

"My buddy called me up and there might be a job opening for me there."

I throw my hands up in defeat. Fan-Freaking-Tastic. Let's top off this whole my-parents-suck-at-being-in-a-relationship scenario with moving in the middle of my senior year of high school. "Are you serious? When would we leave?"

"Probably the beginning of next year. I'm sorry, I know it's not ideal, but your mother really wants a fresh start."

"We can't just move to a different city? We have to move to a whole other state?"

"Your mother doesn't think she can live anywhere near Madelyn."

It takes me a minute to realize who he is talking about. I hadn't heard her name before. My mouth curves in a shape that resembles disgust. He pulls up the website for Missouri State University, "It looks really nice, come on just look at it", as he comes to my side of the table, I know the conversation is over. We're moving.

My friends don't take the news well and three of their parents offer to let me finish out my senior year living with them and I seriously consider it. So many things beg me to stay: a great job that I love, I'm only a semester away from graduating with all my friends and I just started dating a guy I'm thrilled about, Conner. But once again that still small voice nudges me, and I obey.

In a matter of a month, my home is packed away in boxes and I'm saying goodbye to my boyfriend, who promises to come visit me on spring break.

I spend the entirety of the four-day road trip filling my ears with sappy love songs for comfort, trying to reassure myself long distance will work with Connor. Road trips allow for one thing and one thing only: time for thinking. I wonder what our new home will be like, if the people will have an accent or if I'll ever move back to Arizona. Everything I've ever known was in Arizona and I just left it all. The only thing that brings me joy is that I no longer will share a state with my grandparents. The one bright side other than my parents hopefully staying together once and for all.

We get to Missouri December 23rd, 2015. When we arrive, there are movers waiting for us to help usher in the new chapter. I just watch as the men unpack my life with efficiency and indifference. How quickly things can change. Once everything has been brought into the house and the movers have been paid, my parents run out to get food and toilet paper.

"Go ahead and clean out the kitchen please." My mother calls out to us as she shuts the front door.

My brothers and I head to the kitchen and look around. Joe climbs up on the counter to start wiping out the cabinets and I begin opening boxes.

"Hey there's lady bugs in here!"

"What?" Luke and I run over to get a look at the small insect who's living in the cabinet.

Carefully, Joe scoops him up onto a piece of paper and we release him into the wind. But when we return to the cabinet, we find three more in his place. After catching and releasing about twenty ladybugs, we realize we have an infestation on our hands.

"How do we get rid of them all?" I say, frustrated at this added obstacle.

"Why don't we vacuum them out?" Joe brilliantly suggests.

45 minutes later, our vacuum is full of orange lady bugs and our cabinets have been set free from their ladybug oppressors. We finish wiping down all the surfaces before my brothers go upstairs to work on their bedrooms, while I stay to fill the cabinets with plates and cups.

With my hands on my hips, I look fondly over the kitchen that will make our meals for the next couple of years. Maybe life is about to start going right.

A buzzing from my back pocket makes me jump - its Conner.

"Hey!" I greet him in a chipper mood.

"You sound happy, what are you up too?"

We have a long conversation filled with laughs about the ladybug infestation and he tells me about what is happening in Arizona. I'm smiling wide and the sense of hope grows within my soul. We hang up right as my parents walk through the door, grocery bags and toilet paper in hand. They're laughing too and for the first time in a while, I feel like things might be headed in a good direction.

"Hey, call your brothers down here. Let's go to Denny's" My dad smiles, his restored hope reflecting back at me.

. . .

Squished around a small table at Denney's we look like a normal family. We're smiling and laughing. It feels nice. The cloud over us slowly lifting and moving on. My father is in the middle of a story when my phone buzzes. With a smile on my face I look down and see a text from Conner.

"I'm sorry, but I can't come to Missouri with you."

My heart sinks, as I read on. The excuses don't matter to me as he ends his break up text with "I'm sorry".

My eyebrows furrow at the message. We were just on the phone! We were laughing! Everything was good, how can it suddenly have changed? More importantly, how can he break up with me over a text?!

I excuse myself to go to the restroom, before my emotions get the best of me. Grasping the counter to stay standing, I splash water on my face. Who breaks up with someone over a text? Who breaks up with someone over a text a mere thirty minutes after getting off the phone acting like everything is hunky-dory? What a coward!

The anger is a façade to cover the hurt I feel. I look myself in the mirror and take a deep breath. Tears prick the back of my eyes, but I promise myself to keep them caged and fake a smile through the rest of our dinner.

When we get back home, I make a quick escape to my room and let it all out. I try to keep my cries quiet, but some of the sadness demands to be heard and a few screeches escape. It's not too long before there's a knock on the door.

"Are you okay?" my father calls.

"I'll be out in a minute."

After gathering myself together enough to stop the flood pouring from my face, I walk across the hall into my parent's bedroom and tell them everything.

. . .

A month has passed, and I don't feel any better than the night we moved here. In a desperate attempt to escape my misery I start looking for a new job. I print off a handful of resumes and begin driving around the small town I would now call home.

I am careful to avoid the fast food restaurants, for no particular reason I can conjure other than pride. But after the third no in a row, I find myself sitting in a parking lot across the street from a Dairy Queen. As I look at it, I hear a gentle voice inside telling me to drive over and apply. Feeling despaired and defeated, I oblige. I walk in, get an application and before the weekend is over, I have a new job.

. . .

The weather starts to warm up as we get closer to graduation, and all my classmates are talking about is Prom. Even the girls at work are talking about it when I show up for my shift.

"Hey Danielle, do you have a date to the prom?!" Hannah asks me, in her usual bright tone.

"No, I don't really know who I'm going to go with. I might go with a girl from English class."

"You should come with me and my friends! There's 4 of us! You could be my best friend's date!" She's extremely excited and proud of her idea, but my heart skips a beat when she mentions a blind date, and not in the cutesy romantic movie kind of way.

"I don't know…" I trail off as she's pulled away by

a customer.

A few days later, she asks me again about the blind prom date. "We're really going more as a group, but you guys could just match for the pictures and stuff! Come on!" She practically begs me to say yes with her eyes and enthusiasm, but still, I'm nervous.

The conversation drops as she's pulled away by work and I reassure myself I'd be crazy to say yes. It's my senior prom, what if the guy is a jerk? Or worse – expects prom-associated after party activities? I'm enveloped in thought while making an ice cream cone for drive-thru when another voice takes over my thoughts and whispers, "Go say yes."

Almost as if I'm being pushed, I feel my legs carry me over to where Hannah is taking her break and I blurt out "Okay. I'll be your friend's date."

Her smile grows from ear to ear. "Awesome! I'll let Cody know!"

Wedding Day

(20 Years Old)

I watch my brothers and closest friends enter the hall in pairs. They walk in harmony to a song I picked months ago and have since played one hundred times, but this time it sounds better. The rhythm of my heart picks up speed and I whisper for it to stay calm. In circles, my mind repeats itself, "Don't trip, don't trip, don't trip." The last pair of my loved ones enter the hall and I tighten my grip on my father's arm. My stomach is doing flips and despite the fact I've been counting the days until this very moment, I feel like I might puke. The music stops, and my father turns to me.

"That's our cue. Are you ready?"

Time stands still. My breath is gone, and I can't speak. The reality of what I am doing rushes over me. I'm getting married. *I'm* getting married. After everything I've been through, there is man up there who wants to be with me forever. Who knows every dirty little secret and still thinks I'm the one for him. I regain my breath, nod at my dad and we begin to walk.

As we enter the hall the photographer stops us for a moment to take a picture. I smile and tell her to hurry in my mind. When we finally turn to start walking down the aisle, I see him. And my smile is so genuine, so wide, I know I won't be able to feel my cheeks afterwards. Love radiates from my face. I hope he sees it. He doesn't cry like I thought he might. But he looks calm and content, like he is making the best decision of his life right now. And I feel the same.

After a year of long distance while Cody went to college and months of pre-marital counseling, we are here. We are ready. I don't even glance at the audience who's standing for me. Our eyes are fixed on each other and everyone else fades away. The music grows distant and I'm not sure if it has stopped, but I don't care.

When we reach a foot away from the altar, the pastor asks, "Who gives away this bride?"

"Myself and her mother" my father replies.

Cody hugs my father before grabbing my hand and leading me the rest of the way to the altar. Before he drops my hand, he leans in and whispers into my ear, "You look beautiful." My smile is bashful and warm. The pastor tells everyone to take their seats and we begin.

Cody and I had been keeping our vows a secret. I was so excited to hear his, that I was almost giddy when the pastor said, "The couple has prepared their own vows". Cody reaches inside his suit pocket and begins.

"Danielle, I once told you that I love you to the moon and back two times, because once wasn't enough. But now I think back on that and I realize that wasn't completely true. You are a love more than any metaphor can ever try to express. I wake up every morning with joy just to say 'Good Morning' to you. The thought of coming home to you every day for the rest of our lives fills my heart with comfort, happiness and excitement. I turn to God to support me in my desire to be a husband worthy of your love. I promise to never take a day we have together for granted. I promise to stand before you willingly in every storm and in every soaring moment. I promise to, only sometimes though, to let you warm your freezing cold feet on me. I promise to make my life forever yours and build my dreams around you. And most importantly, I promise to love you until our father God brings us home for eternity."

I am in shock of how beautiful the words coming out of his mouth are. When the pastor hands me mine, I almost don't want to read them. But I'm so high up on cloud nine I think my improv would be worse. So, I read them anyways and hope he loves them as much as I loved his.

"Cody, you are my best friend. In you I have found a place where I belong, a place where I'm wanted, a place where I am safe. You understand me like no other person, and you are the one I want to share everything with for the rest of eternity. I can't imagine my life without you. Your hard work and loyalty to not only our relationship, but every relationship you have astounds me and inspires me. And I know that no matter what happens in this life, if I am with you, I will have a home, love and joy. I can't begin to describe to you the incredible blessing it is to have you as my life partner. I am brought to tears when I allow myself to reflect upon how much I love you and the great lengths of love you display for me. And even though it was a roller coaster of a ride to get to you, I wouldn't change a thing if it meant losing you.

So, I take you as you are today, loving who you are now and who you are yet to become. I promise to love you and laugh with you. I promise to grow with you and be your greatest ally. I promise to always fight for you and not against you. I will love you, encourage you, trust you and respect you. I promise to listen to you and learn from you, to support you and accept your support. Most importantly, I promise to have faith in God that he will help us protect and grow our love in all the years to come and through all that life may bring us. So today, in front of all the people that we love, I give myself to you: body, mind and soul. I am yours, forever."

I am crying and can hardly get all the words out. I'm sure that when we leave my makeup will have been washed off by my tears. My vows don't nearly capture enough of my gratitude, but it's best I could do. I am forever in God's debt, and he still brought me a man more incredible than I could've ever imagined.

And suddenly, as messy as the journey was, every confusing day and painful night - I wouldn't change a thing. The painful nights and tireless work to find healing from my trauma. Long distance phone calls that left my heart aching for Cody's touch. The sense of family I had been missing for years. God brought me here. He brought me through it all and he rewarded my obedience and perseverance.

A Note to The Reader

I didn't continue my parent's story to its full extent. So, in case you were wondering, they eventually signed the divorce papers three weeks before my wedding.

As for me, now a honeymoon and house purchase later, my husband and I are living very full lives. We are licensed foster parents and hoping to adopt through the system.

My life wasn't fixed because I got married. I worked hard to find healing from my trauma on my own and before getting married. There's more to life than finding "Happily Ever After", but not being able to find a husband who would love me unconditionally was my biggest fear. My trauma made me terrified I was unlovable. I felt like I would be seen as hand me down garbage after what I'd been through. I was embarrassed and ashamed of my family and where I came from. **But God.** He worked on healing my heart and then he delivered to me my heart's deepest desire. A loving husband, who no matter what I said, couldn't be scared away. A man who has shown me time and time again that he will fight beside me and never leave me.

Because of what happened in this memoir and all the things I left out, (because trust me, there's more) I know God will always provide for me. Even when life gets rough and I feel worn and beaten. When I hold onto God, he delivers me.

The whole reason I wrote this book was to show you this: it doesn't rain forever and when the storm ends, a rainbow will appear.

To that end, I'd like to share with you the lyrics of a song that has gotten me through more tough times than I can count.

Superchick's "Stand in the Rain"

Stand in the rain.

Stand your ground.

Stand up when it's all crashing down.

You stand through the pain.

You won't drown.

And one day, what's lost can be found.

You stand in the Rain.

I believe in you and your ability to survive. Better yet, I believe in God's ability to heal you and bring good out of your circumstance.

From the bottom of my heart, thank you for taking the time to read my story. May you be encouraged and blessed by it.

Love, Danielle Dempsey

Made in the USA
Monee, IL
20 November 2019